Death to Deconstruction

"Deliciously dark, blisteringly honest, and *funny* . . . Like the best art, this book will provoke, not placate; ruffle your feathers, not soothe them; work you up, not calm you down."

John Mark Comer, *New York Times* best-selling author of
The Ruthless Elimination of Hurry and *Live No Lies*

"One thing we need *a lot* more of in our current moment is wise, thoughtful, and pastoral voices stepping into the main conversations we are all having. Josh is one of those voices and this book is one of those conversations. I can see myself buying ten of these and giving them to my entire circle of close friends. It's *that* good."

Jefferson Bethke, *New York Times* best-selling author of
To Hell with the Hustle

"This is not a reactive fundamentalist diatribe against deconstruction. On the contrary, this book deconstructs deconstructionism, offering a blood-and-guts defense of orthodoxy. Yet, at the same time, it is a heart-wrenchingly honest account from someone who deconstructed and returned to tell the tale. This lived experience ensures that this book is a compassionate guide for those wrestling with their faith—faith that has been warped by the American culture, dented by doubt, and hurt by hypocrisy."

Mark Sayers, senior leader of Red Church in Melbourne, Australia,
and author of *Reappearing Church* and *A Non-Anxious Presence*

"Josh Porter is a deeply thoughtful, highly intelligent storyteller who's mastered the art of writing from his bones more than his head. He writes as one who lived in the terrain he walks the reader through, navigating the treacherous journey from deconstruction to faithfulness like a trail guide who knows the land. In *Death to Deconstruction*, he weaves poetic prose, page-turning personal narrative, and deliberate insight into a prophetic call to faithfulness."

Tyler Staton, author of *Searching for Enough* and
Praying Like Monks, Living Like Fools

"There is much being written on deconstruction these days, but the vast majority is coming from the outside looking in written by observers and spectators rather than those who have lived among the rubble of deconstruction. Josh writes as an insider, a wrestler with God, church, life, all of it—which makes his voice not just unique but credible. If you're going on a journey through your own deconstruction, you need a credible guide. You will identify with his frustrations and be challenged by some narrow paths he recommends, but he will lead you to the real Jesus who is more radical, more rebellious, more tolerant, and more unwavering than popular podcast personalities dare to have you believe. If you want Jesus and not an off-ramp from faith, read this book."

Rick McKinley, author of *Faith for This Moment* and
This Beautiful Mess, and founding pastor of
Imago Dei Community

"As leaders at Van City Church, we've had the privilege of witnessing Josh learn and grow with humility as he follows Jesus and helps lead others to do so. He has demonstrated his ability and character not only to teach our specific church but to speak about deconstruction and fidelity to Jesus to the broader church and those far from God. As our friend, we celebrate with him as he uses his gifts to honor King Jesus."

The Overseers, Van City Church in Vancouver, WA

**Foreword by
John Mark Comer**

Death to Deconstruction

RECLAIMING FAITHFULNESS
AS AN ACT OF REBELLION

Joshua S. Porter

KREGEL
PUBLICATIONS

Published by Kregel Publications, a division of Kregel Inc., 2450 Oak Industrial Dr. NE, Grand Rapids, MI 49505. www.kregel.com.

The persons and events portrayed in this book have been used with permission. To protect the privacy of these individuals, some names and identifying details have been changed.

The authors and publisher are not engaged in rendering medical or psychological services, and this book is not intended as a guide to diagnose or treat medical or psychological problems. If medical, psychological, or other expert assistance is required, the reader should seek the services of a health-care provider or certified counselor.

Scriptures taken from the Holy Bible, New International Version®, NIV®. Copyright © 1973, 1978, 1984, 2011 by Biblica, Inc.™ Used by permission of Zondervan. All rights reserved worldwide. www.zondervan.com. The "NIV" and "New International Version" are trademarks registered in the United States Patent and Trademark Office by Biblica, Inc.™

The author is represented by MacGregor & Luedeke.

Cataloging-in-Publication Data available from the Library of Congress.

ISBN 978-0-8254-4734-1, print
ISBN 978-0-8254-7789-8, epub
ISBN 978-0-8254-6941-1, Kindle

Printed in the United States of America
22 23 24 25 26 27 28 29 30 31 / 5 4 3 2 1

For Beck.
When your time
comes, rebel well.

CONTENTS

"When I was young, I believed in three things: Marxism, the redemptive power of cinema, and dynamite. Now I just believe in dynamite."

SERGIO LEONE

"When I was a child, I talked like a child, I thought like a child, I reasoned like a child. When I became a man, I put the ways of childhood behind me."

1 CORINTHIANS 13:11

FOREWORD

THE CHRISTIAN MYSTIC THOMAS Merton once said that the best art "enables us to find ourselves and lose ourselves at the same time."[1]

It's no surprise, then, that my friend Josh Porter started out as a fire-breathing, fake-blood-spewing lead singer of a punk rock band[2] . . . an *artist*.

Twenty years on, Josh is still an artist.

The book you're about to read—part Mary Karr–esque memoir, deliciously dark, blisteringly honest, and *funny*; part erudite intellectual tour of the dominant theological and sociological roots underneath the growing social phenomenon of deconstruction—is, like the best art, designed to provoke something *in* you, to draw out a gut-level emotional reaction. Josh is like a good friend from his rural Georgian past, grabbing your wrist after a snakebite and sucking the poison out of your body before it hits your bloodstream and kills you.

You see, Josh has become something more than an artist; he's become a pastor too, working on the canvas of the soul. His art has always been provocative, even polarizing at times. I assume Josh would say that's on purpose. But it's not for shock-jaw entertainment to draw a crowd, or a subtle play to garner more followers on the very platforms he is criticizing (proof: Josh is straight edge about social media too . . .). It's to shock our *heart* before it dies of spiritual arrhythmia.

Josh's word for this is "rebellion." (See the subtitle.) At first, I bristled a bit at his word choice. Isn't "rebellion" a snake-in-the-garden thing? As he writes, "We think of uprisings and rebellions, and we think of protests, riots, Molotov cocktails. But often, the most subversive and effective rebellion is the simple defiant act of telling a different story."

The book you are about to read is an act of rebellion, of telling a different, far better story than the dominant, millennial narratives of our age.

Both Josh and I came up playing in bands, and I imagine we carried some of our artistic sensibilities over into our preaching and writing. But while our paths have a common origin, they also diverge. While Josh was lighting cymbals on fire in seedy bars, I was trying to rip off this new band called Coldplay. Josh was fighting "the system"; I was trying to game it.

Decisions about mascara-wearing men aside, Josh and I became fast friends many years ago, when he moved to Portland. We worked together for a good run at Bridgetown Church, and his thoughtfulness and theological acumen gave a helpful sharpening to my own thinking. But it's not his IQ, wit, or extraordinary writing talent that drew me to Josh; it's his level of allegiance to Jesus as Lord, *and his rebellion against all the other lords of the world.*

The world around us—and often, sadly, even our fellow Christians—often pull us *down* to a lower level of allegiance, to let a little self-worship slide . . . wink-wink. Very few call us *up*, to a greater holiness.

Those who do are our true friends.

The best-seller lists abound with books by former Christians, and your local Christian bookstore is likely stocked with entire shelves of "Christian lite." That's okay; it's nothing new.

But *this* is not *that.*

This book will provoke, not placate; ruffle your feathers, not soothe them; work you up, not calm you down. It will call you up, if you let it.

—John Mark Comer

(Before We Begin)

IN THE SPRING OF 2018, I decided to kill myself. I opened a notebook and made a list. I split the list into two columns: pros and cons. I didn't want to be one of those hasty suicides. I needed to figure this out.

Mostly, though, my mind was made up.

I counted the items in each column: eight pro, seven con. Simple math.

There were, to my estimation, many pragmatic benefits to killing myself, but there were also some grave consequences that ranged from disastrous trauma for my loved ones to minor inconveniences like having to call someone to figure out my life insurance coverage. There were details to iron out. It was starting to sound like a lot of work. I wondered, "If I kill myself on a Wednesday, who will preach the sermon at church the following Sunday?"

I was, after all, the pastor.

I priced something called an "exit bag" online. My stomach was starting to hurt. I wrote in the "con" column: *I will bring shame to the name of Jesus.* This was important to me as a Christian. Do Christians kill themselves? I thought of something Brennan Manning wrote in his memoir, "Things haven't turned out the way I'd planned." Sitting in my church office price-checking helium kits with which to stop my heart and brain, I thought, "Things are not turning out the way I'd planned."

I frowned at the list. I was not doing well. I had come to believe a series of pretty nasty lies that would require a lot of hard work to undo. I sincerely believed with all my heart that my dying was probably the best option for everyone.

Probably.

Squatting like a gargoyle on the edge of the abyss, deceived, but with enough self-awareness to realize I was blowing it, I thought of something Thomas Merton said: "Despair is the absolute extreme of self-love. It is reached when a person deliberately turns his back on all help from anyone else in order to taste the rotten luxury of knowing himself to be lost."[1]

There was no clinical depression, no Lifetime movie tragedy. It started when I'd allowed years of unaddressed self-loathing and despair to snowball for a few lonely, dark months. Then I found myself weeping as I prayed through Psalm 69, desperate and miserable, and even with no one around to see it, I was pretty embarrassed by the whole thing.

What a joke, I remember thinking.

Killing myself, I knew, represented the utter undoing of everything I believed and the complete failure of everything to which I had dedicated my life, a catastrophe, a spiraling explosion of flaming wreckage. I didn't believe that killing myself was permissible, but I thought of it the way Just War types rationalize killing Nazis. Sure, Jesus told us not to kill people, but sometimes you just have to do it.

It was hard to capture the magnitude of this awareness in a list of cons. One line item basically covered it: *I will bring shame to the name of Jesus.*

By this, I guess I meant that I had dedicated my life to learning and teaching the Bible and theology, to advocating for and practicing the way of Jesus, that I had built up the entirety of my life around Jesus and his teaching, and I was prepared to burn the entire thing to the ground, to reveal myself a selfish coward, a phony, a liar.

I imagined someone having to explain to my church, "Sorry, but the pastor turned out to be a huckster, week by week peddling a hope in Jesus he didn't actually have. You'd all be fools to believe it yourselves."

Like many, many people I'd known, it looked like I was giving up on Jesus.

I counted the items in each column again.

Part One

DECONSTRUCTING GOD

"There was nothing left to do but remain in the valley and suffer, or pack up and leave for more sunny climes and so live in guilt and shame forever."

—NICK CAVE, *AND THE ASS SAW THE ANGEL*

Chapter 1

BLOOD AND FIRE

ON THE SATURDAY THAT my faith began to erode, my friend tells me, "I don't want to blow fire anymore."

We go on in minutes, and only now is he telling me this.

"Dude," he says, "look at this." He runs a couple of fingers between his lips, probes his gums, then presents me with a wet, gray pulp.

"What's that?" I ask.

"My *gums*, dude. The rubbing alcohol is melting them or something."

I lift the bottle from the dressing room counter and squint at the label. It doesn't say anything about melting gums.

"Just don't swallow it," I tell him.

"I'm not, man. But still."

When you're eighteen years old, turning your local punk rock band into a fire-breathing spectacle isn't rocket science. The routine is simple: (1) We duct tape an old T-shirt to the end of a drumstick. (2) We douse the stick's shirt-end in rubbing alcohol so that when we apply fire, it becomes a crude torch. (3) Our friend Jesse (who isn't actually *in* the band) takes a long drag from the rubbing alcohol—fills his cheeks with the stuff—and when we hit that first dramatic chord of our set (an E minor) Jesse spews the rubbing alcohol at the lit torch like seawater from a whale's blowhole, igniting a flaming red nebula that seemed, if we were honest, pretty dangerous and likely in violation of any number of fire and safety codes—even at scummy bars like this one. While Jesse spewed circus performer flames, our drummer used a similar approach to set his entire drum kit on fire. This is why we never briefed anyone on our amateur pyrotechnics. Better to ask for forgiveness than permission.

"Just do it one more time," I reason, hitching up my leather shorts.

Jesse frowns at the bottle and sighs.

"Besides," I say, "it's not like *I* can do it. I'm spitting blood at the same time." I produce the bottle of dyed corn syrup, and Jesse sighs again. Thing is, on most nights, while our drummer was setting his kit on fire and Jesse was blowing fire over the crowd, the rest of the band filled their mouths with a homemade batch of faux blood so everyone wound up looking like Sissy Spacek in the third act of *Carrie*.

"You guys do fire," I say, pointing at Jesse and our drummer, "and the rest of us do blood."

Mike, who plays guitar, grimaces. "That corn syrup tastes disgusting."

"At least it doesn't melt your gums," Jesse points out.

Mike shrugs. "Touché, I guess."

"You guys ready?" I shout at the band. "Let's pray."

SHOWTIME

Sticky with sweat and fake blood, I'm screaming into a dented microphone, rolling and gyrating on a filthy stage in a half-empty dive bar.

I'm singing songs I wrote about Jesus.

EIGHTEEN YEARS AFTER SHOWTIME

The problem, for me, was that I'd been raised by a Christian culture to be grafted into that Christian culture, and as far as I could tell, a lot of it was a sham. The Bible, I'd been told, was the nonnegotiable standard issue manual for the whole thing, but it didn't read much like a manual at all. Not a good one, anyway. For starters, the same stories showed up all over the place, but no one bothered making the details agree with each other. One guy writes, "X amount of people did this thing over here," but then when another guy tells the story, he writes, "It was actually a totally different number in a totally different place."

I figured one guy rounded up and the other rounded down, whatever. But that was only the beginning of it. If I was honest, some of the Bible's factoids weren't exactly what I'd call reliable. The Bible's world, for example, was supported by planetary columns and surrounded by a dome of water. And for every weird water dome there were two more details that I could only describe as morally reprehensible. Babies smashed against rocks. Disobedient children stoned to death. Holy war.

I figured maybe I don't get it. I'll just do my best to follow the rules. There were a lot of them, and to hear these people in the Bible talk about it, they were pretty important. Problem was, I was terrible at that. Inwardly, I was often miserable over my own failure, wracked with grief, driven crazy by my ineptitude. I'd go looking for the merciful Jesus of my youth group, the one willing to let most anything slide just as long as you prayed a magical forgiveness incantation at summer camp.

"Jesus, I believe you died on the cross for my sins. I invite you into my heart as my personal Lord and Savior."

(I couldn't find a prayer like this one or instructions on how to offer it anywhere in the Bible, but I had it on the good authority of just about every Christian in my known world that avoiding hell more or less boiled down to reciting this magic formula.)

Then there were the Christians.

Just about every Christian I'd ever known in my first couple of decades alive was either wholly or in part pretty lousy at the whole Christian thing. Growing up in the rural Deep South, every fervent White churchgoer in my life was shamelessly racist and heatedly nationalistic. As a kid, my church's summer Bible camp began with the Pledge of Allegiance to the American flag. The sermons I remember were about the abomination of homosexuality, the corrupting poison of rock and roll music, the unspeakable horror of being left behind when God zapped every Christian into heaven during the rapture (any day now).

The Christianity I knew didn't remind me much of the stuff I read in the New Testament. When I asked about it, I was warned against questions in general, as they tended to cause the one asking to "go liberal." When I pointed at things like one set of numbers that contradicted another, the Christians urged me to "just have faith." If I asked about the Bible's near-constant emphasis on caring for the poor and the oppressed, I was told to tread carefully. "You're starting to sound like a socialist."

"Who are you to question God?" they'd ask.

The faith I could muster didn't seem to change much. I was getting sad. People were asking, "Well, are you in sin?" They'd ask, "Do you have enough faith?"

I wasn't sure. Maybe?

There was another big problem: me.

I don't like being told what to do. I don't like homogeneity; everyone made to look and talk and think and behave the same way. I don't like doing things according to modes of obligatory tradition. I don't like rules for rules' sake. What I really want to do is defy these things. Defy homogeneity, defy obligatory tradition, defy rules for rules' sake.

Tangled somewhere in the unforgiving thorns of my culturally Christian world was Jesus. My *idea* of Jesus, anyway. I liked my idea of Jesus, but I couldn't much see a way to free him from the awful mess of church, the Bible, and Christianity itself.

I figured maybe I'll have to make up my own Christianity.

TWELVE HOURS BEFORE SHOWTIME

We also prayed before rehearsal. Praying is what "Christian bands" do. With a few hours left before we had to load the van and head to

Savannah, I asked the room, "Who wants to pray before we start?" Someone always volunteered. They'd pray that when we got where we were going and when we performed and when we were offstage, we would represent Jesus well.

Our rehearsal space was the master bedroom of a dilapidated mobile home where a few of us lived. This was important to me. I'd dropped out of high school and abandoned the middle-class comforts of my parents' home in service to the dream. The dream: living in a ramshackle trailer and playing music throughout the local dive bar scene of the swampy Deep South. Now, you had to speak up if you were the one praying to compete with the low drone of the half-dozen box fans crowding the stiff, filthy carpet. We'd carried all the furniture out of the bedroom months ago to make space for drums and amplifiers, and the room's former residents were moved down the hall to mattresses on the floor. During the move, a couch had become wedged in the hallway a few feet above the ground. When our combined efforts were helpless to budge it, we left it hanging there until we moved.

The windows had all been covered in aluminum foil to reflect the merciless Georgia sun, but that didn't help much. Scattered garbage and dirty laundry covered most surfaces. An authentic coffin we'd rescued from the dumpster behind a nearby funeral home was our living room coffee table. Everything stank. People worried about us.

Inside, we were praying.

This weird thing we were about to do, we believed, had everything to do with God. That's how it all started, anyway. Lately, it seemed as if we were teetering, the scales of spirituality tipping, and I was sliding away from everything, poised to topple headlong into apostasy.

ELEVEN HOURS AFTER SHOWTIME

At church the next morning, I knew people were looking at me funny. I had flaking eyeliner caked in the corners of my eyes, and later that afternoon, I'd realize there were gobs of dried corn syrup stuck in the teased brambles of my hair.

A man I'd known all my life approached me, his face a cheerless mask, as if the sight of me was so deeply troubling that he could not affect the superficiality of Southern kindness.

"I want you to know, Josh," he told me, shaking my hand, "that I pray for you all the time."

He looked pained saying it, his eyes pleading, wanting to pull me back from the heresy written all over my face.

"Thanks," was all I said.

I was raised going to church. The same church every Sunday. Aside from a penchant for asking questions and an obvious disdain for traditionalism, at eighteen, I'd given no indication that I had any plans to abandon my Christianity. Unlike many of my more presentable peers (the ones who *didn't* show up to church speckled with mascara and fake blood), I'd demonstrated a completely uncoerced enthusiasm for allowing my faith to guide what I was sure would become my life's work: a fire-breathing punk rock band, with all of its rigorous demands. Like living in a dilapidated trailer with no air-conditioning.

But this, to the religious bubble of Southeast Georgia, was more worrying than a brush with atheism.

Shaking this man's hand in the church of my childhood, I thought of how I had seen the same disapproving glower on his face a week earlier when two Black teenagers passed the church on a Wednesday evening. He sighed then like he was sighing now as he broke conversation to monitor their passing, saying, "Hang on, I want to make sure these *brothers* aren't up to anything." This guy's own nefarious racism bothered him much less than the unbearable knowledge that I'd been wearing makeup in my band, a contrast that, in many ways, exemplified the Christian culture of my upbringing.

That Sunday, other young men smiled and shook hands with happy, approving elders. I knew these other teenagers. They preferred loose sex and weekend keggers to rock concerts, but they cleaned up real nice, and hey, they played football and tucked their shirts in and showed decidedly less evidence of mascara or fake blood in their perfectly coifed hair.

One of them—the former president of the youth group before he graduated to leading men's Bible studies—joined the old man's scowl when he saw me.

"Still playing in that band, Josh?" he asked.

"Yeah."

He cuffed me on the shoulder with a sigh. "We're all praying for you."

ONE WEEK AFTER SHOWTIME

Footage from that evening's performance would later feature in a short film about my band's conflict with the Southern Baptist church where we grew up but were eventually discouraged from attending. The little video had been a homework assignment for a local film school student who followed our band's weird story. In the footage, we do—I must admit—make easy targets of ourselves.

There I am, shirtless, covered in fake blood, screaming, convulsing on stage. The footage overlays an interview with one of the pastors who was instrumental in my quasi excommunication from the church that reared me.

"Biblically," the pastor says, "I don't know if their style of music would hold up to God's standards."[1]

All the distinctive features of a solid deconversion story were there: conservative fundamentalist upbringing, an abused and weaponized Bible, hypocrisy, rejected by religious authority. But there I am, covered in fake blood, surrounded by reckless plumes of fire, singing about Jesus. The Jesus I knew back then.

DECONVERSION BY SELFIE

On July 26, 2019, a once-famous Christian author and pastor posted a photo of himself on Instagram. So far, nothing unusual.

In it, he looks out into a beautiful wilderness. Here were all the curated staples of the comrade-approved social media post: lush scenery, a blue sky, a mountain, the person doing the posting awkwardly cramming themselves into the image, acting natural, leaving the beholder to wonder: Wait, so did he just ask someone, here, take a picture of me staring at this mountain while I pretend to look at it?

Again, all very normal.

The other, more sinister Instagram staple is also accounted for: the crumbling veneer of forced (and dishonest) positivity. The photo's caption admits that the author has lost his faith, is divorcing his wife (shattering the family that housed their children), and all of this as a big, bold, beautiful adventure!

Here I am in the picture, he seems to say, the story of me! Things may *look* like they're coming apart at the seams, but really, they are quite wonderful! Better than ever, actually! My ex-wife is better than ever! Our kids are better than ever! *I'm* better than ever! Get a load of this view! If it bothers you, it's only because you are—unlike the new, more enlightened me—still trapped in the backward obsolescence of religion.

Deconversion by selfie.

The rest of the feed follows suit: smiling selfies in front of murals, breathless selfies at marathons, pensive selfies before white brick walls. Each with flowery prose about the good life, a life without Jesus, the great, brave adventure of it all.

Deconversion brand management.

Describing his parting with Jesus, the former pastor wrote: "The popular phrase for this is 'deconstruction,' the biblical phrase is 'falling away.'"[2]

I've been watching a similar turn of events for most of my life: Jesus as fad diet. Really important until it isn't. I have beheld legions of fevered converts brought up in Christian households and churned out by youth cultures and camps. Stirred to frenzy by what may have been genuine encounters with God, they ran, and they ambled along the road of discipleship until they fell prey to the Great Predators that stalk the dark ravines lining the narrow way—shadowy brutes that prey on pain and confusion, making meals of once-eager Christians.

THE GREAT PREDATORS

The first Great Predator is *biblical illiteracy*. Although the Bible is an ancient library of writings drafted by dozens of authors across multiple continents in several languages, over several centuries, the most complex literary volume in history is usually perused like some simple, superficial thing and dismissed by angry readers who don't understand the passages that so offend them. Who can blame them? They've never been taught how to read it.

The second Great Predator is *the problem of evil*. If God is so good, and powerful enough to do anything, why is there so much evil, injustice, and suffering in the world? Of all the Great Predators, this one is the most cunning. It lures its prey from the narrow road by traumatizing them, and in their pain, they become convinced that they can go no further.

The third Great Predator is a *politicized Christianity*. When oppressive, power-hungry bullies seem part and parcel of Christian experience, who can blame the great many who want nothing to do with the ugly mob of mean-spirited, hyperpolitical Bible-thumpers?

The fourth Great Predator is *hypocrisy*. It's not just the seedy pockets of church history (crusades and colonists, Jim Crow, the prosperity gospel). It often seems as if those most ardent about Christian morality are the least likely to uphold it. If it's not the sex scandals and embezzlement of televangelists, it's the indulgent Instagram lifestyles of influential pastors, or the casual racism of a churchgoing family member, or the generally unkind face of evangelicalism.

The final lumbering Predator is *self-denial*. Even if you get past the politicians and hypocrites, even if you survive your great tragedy with your faith intact, you will find that it all comes down to Jesus, whose invitation to apprenticeship was "deny yourself." Modern Western individualists cannot abide so outrageous a demand. In our Diet

Coke world of #dowhatmakesyouhappy, the audacity of Jesus's call to self-denial isn't just bold, it's backward, bigoted, and dangerous.

Biblical illiteracy, the problem of evil, politicized Christianity, hypocrisy, and self-denial. The Great Predators. I fell to each of them.

Eventually, I decided to stagger upright and hobble forward.

THE THREE READERS

This book has three readers. If you have some experience with Jesus, with Christianity, you're one of them. You're probably saying to yourself, maybe I'm not, but you are.

The First Reader is the Quivering Disciple. You follow Jesus. You love him. Either you grew up around the things of Jesus, or you discovered them somewhere along the snaking, chaotic road of life, but here you are. No disciple of Jesus—not Mary Magdalene nor the apostle Paul, not Harriet Tubman nor C. S. Lewis—managed to execute their apprenticeship to Jesus standing bolt upright, back rigid, a cool beacon of uninterrupted, stoic confidence. Mostly, we're pretty bad at it, give or take. Simon Peter denied Jesus. Paul called himself the first and foremost sinner. Both of them followed Jesus. They were, like you, First Reader, Quivering Disciples who sometimes walked the narrow road of discipleship with joy and steely resolve, and probably just as often dragged themselves deeper still, limping, bedraggled, trembling beneath the weight of it all, but dragging themselves deeper still.

The Second Reader is the Deconstructed. The term "deconstruction" has all sorts of unique contexts and meanings, but the basic definition of the verb sums it up:

> **de·con·struct** | ˌdēkənˈstrəkt | verb [*with object*] **1** : analyze (a text or a linguistic or conceptual system) by deconstruction, typically in order to expose its hidden internal assumptions and contradictions and subvert its apparent significance or unity **2** : reduce (something) to its constituent parts in order to reinterpret it

At the time of writing, the term "deconstruction" has become an umbrella term to describe a process in which someone who was once a Christian embarks on a quest to jettison their Christianity. Bailing out on God isn't exactly a bold new concept; it's been going on since the origins of Christianity and earlier, but the modern junk drawer term "deconstruction" probably has some roots in something called critical theory, a philosophical tradition that "refuses to identify freedom with any institutional arrangement or fixed system of thought."[3]

Deconstruction is an ambiguous wraith that moves through all manner of progressive ideologies, consuming and reshaping them like No-Face in Hayao Miyazaki's *Spirited Away*. The spirit of deconstruction is often born from healthy and reasonable questions and doubt but piloted by frustration and hurt. It roves the endless chambers of existential angst, gobbling up anything to relieve the pain and to hurt the people who hurt it.

Because deconstruction rises from the shapeless tar of critical theory, it is often suspicious of any and all forms of structure and authority as inherently oppressive. Thus, deconstruction wants no master beyond itself, creating a colossal arrangement of near-impenetrable hyperindividualism. This is a very American thing to do. As theologian Greg Boyd once put it, "If the fall is about humans wanting to be independent lords of our own lives, then America is the fall on steroids!"[4]

Sometimes the deconstruction creature retains incomplete scraps and fragments of Christianity (usually, the parts that suit the deconstructing party's evolving ideology, until they don't), but without authority, this patchwork worldview becomes a muddled snarl of all-you-can-eat belief—a loaded, nauseating tray of fried spirituality. Each morsel looked delicious at the buffet, but it doesn't exactly make for a sensible meal.

Deconstruction is the shadow of transformation. As they grow and mature, every disciple of Jesus will transform their theology, their faith, their belief, in several significant ways and in many small ones. We learn we were wrong about certain things. Stuff we thought was really important becomes decidedly less so. Some things we undervalued become key. We learn to understand things in different ways. But all of this is an evolution of the same faith. We may renovate the house of our discipleship, move things around, paint a few walls, get rid of some old furniture, but it remains the same recognizable house.

Every disciple of Jesus transforms. Transformation unfolds within the safeguards of *orthodoxy*—the accumulated wisdom and accountability of many centuries of the Jesus movement that discerns what teaching and practice align with Jesus and what departs from him. Orthodoxy has room for transformation, but deconstruction scraps orthodoxy, stripping it for spare parts.

Deconstruction is an aggressive, cancerous outgrowth of the ordinary transforming we all do, but it takes a sledgehammer to the walls in a desperate, scrambling effort to reveal some sinister rot within. Deconstruction is a takedown, not an evolution. It's not a little squirming tadpole that sprouts legs and drags itself up a primordial beach—one thing becoming a new thing, but still the same thing—it brings an angry boot down on the slippery-limbed fish before its gills take their first gulp of oxygen. Sometimes it happens fast, beginning in a moment and accomplished with quiet efficiency. Other times it takes months or years, but eventually, renovating the house proves too tiring, and the decision is made to tear the entire structure from its foundation so that the old house is deconstructed and no more.

"The popular phrase for this is 'deconstruction,' the biblical phrase is 'falling away.'"

You, Second Reader, the Deconstructed, you're wary of all this. You're wise to the con. But let me admit something: I'm not trying to change your mind. Why would I? We probably have the same story, more or less.

The Third Reader is the One at the Impasse. You follow Jesus, and you have arrived at the end of the first road. The time has come to either transform or deconstruct.

You don't know if you need a paintbrush or a sledgehammer.

ABANDON ALL HOPE YE WHO ENTER HERE

The thing we often call "Christianity" can be a trying way of life. This is by design. Jesus, founder of the movement, warned his would-be followers that what he had in mind would be difficult, that we'd lose much, that much would be asked of us, that friends and family might fall away in the process, that there would be people who would hate us and want to do us harm for no other reason than being in league with Jesus. There are very understandable reasons that when many are confronted with Jesus's jarring invitation to "deny yourself, take up your cross, and follow me," they decline (see Luke 9:23). I was given every conceivable reason to abandon the Christian ship. I'll tell you about them. There are very understandable reasons that many who responded to the strange call of Jesus in one season of life scorn it in another. But there are other, arguably *less* valid reasons for falling away.

Everyone knows someone who is formerly Christian. It could be someone you've read about, someone you love; it could be you. In my personal experience with the Great Predators and through deconstruction, I've found that logic and candid, straightforward sincerity are not hallmarks of the deconstruction dialogue, nor its frenzied religious pushback. Christians are scared and disappointed to see their brothers and sisters deconstruct their faith. Pastors and parents are troubled by common doubts and misgivings about the Bible and the church. Jaded former Christians are often embittered by the violent process of deconversion, becoming aggressive and combative in their new worldview. A wall is erected between the past and the present. Any conversation devolves into defense mode for fear of toppling a flimsy ideology under the weight of its own hypocrisy.

But I get deconstruction. I understand deconversion.

I've already given away that I somehow moved from deconstruction, through disenchantment, back to following Jesus. It's in the not-so-subtle title of the book and everything. But I did not return to faith because I was afraid of what other people would think if I didn't. I am wired for rebellion. To a fault, I am compelled to defy what is asked and expected of me. I do not persist in faith because I am afraid of being punished if I don't. I dispensed with all my weird ideas of God as a menacing vendor of cosmic hellfire a long time ago. I do not insist on the Christian tradition because I need a job. Though I chose to become a pastor, the task isn't exactly a picnic, and there are lots of other things I could be doing. I certainly did not embrace the way of Jesus by plugging my ears and closing my eyes to very real, very valid problems with God, the Bible, and the church. I obsessed over them for years. I read and I studied. I searched.

I was a Christian. I embarked on a path toward deconstruction. I am still a Christian.

These things will become increasingly clear as we go, but for clarity's sake, I'll put my cards on the table: I believe in the triune God of the Bible. I believe in the God whom Jesus called "Father." I believe that Jesus of Nazareth is, as he put it, "the way, and the truth, and the life" (John 14:6). I believe that no one comes to the Father except through Jesus. I believe that the Spirit of Jesus continues to equip, direct, transform, and convict disciples of Jesus today. I believe that the Bible is inspired by God, and as such, it is trustworthy and authoritative in everything it intends to say and to teach. Understanding what the Bible intends to say and teach is complicated and divisive, so the Bible is often misunderstood and abused. I believe that the only venue for carrying out discipleship to Jesus and for learning and obeying the Scriptures is the imperfect but beautiful gathering together of Christians that we call the church.

Having navigated both enthusiastic churchgoing evangelicalism and disillusioned alienation from it, I'm not interested in pandering to a fragile Christianity that doesn't make room for our serious quibbles, critiques, and crises. I find it equally unhelpful to placate the happily deconverted by behaving as if their post-Christian spirituality is without its own set of contradictions. If spirituality and our questions about it matter at all, we should probably use the same shrewd measuring stick to appraise being Christian *and* not being Christian.

Whatever you are, reading this thing will be anything but a comfortable or accommodating experience. This book won't pat you on the head, and it won't work very hard to avoid offending you or calling your most beloved preconceptions into question. I'm well beyond concern for any of those things. If you are not willing to be provoked, to have your most cherished ideological infrastructure called into question, whether it is Christian or post-Christian, then abandon all hope ye who enter here.

The Apprentice: A Troublesome Book

THE YOUNG APPRENTICE WAS raised amongst monks and lapsed sages. They told the young Apprentice, "You must choose for yourself a master."

The Apprentice wondered aloud, "Won't I follow the same master under whose teaching I have been raised?"

But the sages told him, "You must make that decision for yourself."

"If I decide to follow the Master, how do I follow him?"

One of the old sages, bent and bruised from a lifetime of his own apprenticeship, leveled a single trembling finger at two paths that opened before them. The first road was wide and accommodating, its terrain a flat and even blanket of soft green grass. The sky was bright blue and cloudless overhead. A homely wooden sign marked the path. On its gnarled, weathered surface was fixed a single word: Death.

To the left, the second road was nothing like the first. Tight and winding, overgrown thorns and brambles lining both sides, a canopy of leafless branches enclosing overhead like a tapestry of splintering bone. It was dark and foreboding and set before it was a sign not unlike the first in appearance but written across it was a different word: Life.

The lapsed sage said, "If you choose to follow him, the Master will lead you and be with you on the road that leads to life."

The Apprentice was afraid. He said, "The Master's road scares me. The other road looks easier to travel."

"It is," the sage told him. "But it leads to death."

"I am afraid that if I walk the Master's road, I might die."

"You will. Then you will live."

"Suppose I should choose *no* masters?"

"All of us choose masters. All other masters you will find on the wide, bright road."

"Suppose I walk the frightening road, how can I know the Master's teaching, that I may find my way?"

"Through his Word. It is written, and he will write it again on your heart."

"How can I trust that what is written is the Master's Word?"

"The Master has entrusted his Word to scribes, elders, artists, poets, and playwrights. The Master himself has preserved his trustworthy Word."

"How can a perfect Master author his Word through imperfect writers?"

"This you must learn."

"Can I have proof?"

"No. You cannot."

The Apprentice looked at the harrowing road again and asked, "How can I know that I have read the Master's Word well?"

"Generations of readers have come before you. The Master's Word is not read alone but in the company of generations of readers past and present. Their prayerful vigilance and centuries of study will help guide and protect you so that you will not wander from the truth of what is written."

"What if I do not like what is written?"

"Sometimes you will not. The truth is not safe, and it will not bend to your will."

"Other sages have told me that the Master's Word is a simple book of rules without secret or mystery, that it simply says what it says."

The old sage only laughed.

"What if I refuse to obey his Word?"

"You are not the Master's prisoner. You are his beloved. You may follow the Master's Word, or you may reject it. If you seek the Master's Word, you will find trouble, but you will also find the truth."

The Apprentice asked, "Can I follow the Master without the Master's Word?"

The sage said, "No."

The Apprentice opened the book and began to read.

THE FIRST GREAT PREDATOR: BIBLICAL ILLITERACY

"There are worse crimes than burning books. One of them is not reading them."

—JOSEPH BRODSKY

Chapter 2

POLITICAL CARTOONS AND
RATTLESNAKE WORSHIP

JUST UP THE ROAD, I'd been told, there was one of those churches where they handle rattlesnakes, and immediately I'm jealous. They pass them around like party favors, the snakes, and you might just go into a trance while holding one, eyes rolled back, convulsing, the whole thing.

I'd also heard these venomous rattlesnakes occasionally bite the snake-handling churchgoers. Of course they did. They were rattle-snakes. My brother and I, having grown up in rural Georgia, we knew that when you go walking through the woods and you hear the menacing rattle of an Eastern Diamondback, you run in the other direction, full tilt. But these guys, I was told, they would just reach into a straw-lined crate and grab these big coiling serpents by the tail while an organist bangs out another verse of "Amazing Grace." They keep these snake-filled crates right there in the church building.

My church didn't even have a fishbowl.

So, when (not *if* but *when*) you got bit, God would test you. If you chicken out and stagger to the local emergency room, bloated, turning purple, then you fail the test, and you can no longer attend the Sunday snake party. But if you really believe God will see you through the whole snakebite ordeal—*really* believe it—then God will dry the venom in your veins before it stops your heart, and you get to become a spiritual superhero, emerging victorious from the poisonous maw of the serpent. All this they got from the Bible. Sort of.

Nothing this exciting ever happened at my church.

SUNDAY MORNING IN 1989

On a Sunday morning in 1989, my dad switched on the lights in the wood-paneled room I shared with my older brother. The sun was up, and I could hear Fine Young Cannibals' "She Drives Me Crazy" coming from the radio in the kitchen because my parents liked the top 40 station for the morning, the kind where the DJ keeps saying in his DJ voice, "You're listening to Mix 97.3!"

"Y'all get up," my dad says. "Get dressed."

He doesn't have to tell us what we're getting dressed for, it's Sunday morning. Sunday mornings are always the same.

My brother and I, we'd squint and groan and pull the covers over our heads to shield our delicate, sleep-hungry eyes from the cruel light. Sure, our friends were at church, some nice people we'd known all our lives, but we didn't *want* to go to church any more than we *wanted* to go to school.

Sunday mornings are always the same. Here's how you get ready for church: You drag your uncooperative body from the bedroom to the kitchen and reach for one of the blueberry muffins your mother baked while you were still sleeping. You listen for your parents, making sure they can't hear you, and you turn the dial on the Zenith tube TV, clicking through static-punctuated local programming, adjusting the antenna to get a better picture. But your dad, he probably walks in. Probably, he says, "No TV. Get dressed." So, you sit there eating a blueberry muffin, and the radio starts playing "Sara" by Starship and you bum hard.

Church was the only occasion for which our family required formal attire. My dad wore a tie, my mom put on a dress before she curled my little sister's hair. My brother and I begrudgingly tucked our collared button-ups into our khaki slacks. Everyone looked ridiculous because none of us actually dressed this way under normal circumstances. Normally, my dad wore NASCAR T-shirts and flip-flops. My parents would never let me wear my favorite Ghostbusters shirt on a Sunday morning. Sunday night, maybe, but never Sunday morning.

We were told that the Bible said you give God your best, and by this, it apparently meant that thousands of years following the time of writing, people in another culture on another continent were required to sport ties and dresses to Sunday church meetings despite the fact that no one writing the Bible had ever seen a tie in the first place. What else could it have meant?

So, you make yourself uncomfortable, and you go sit through an hour of Sunday school, then you sit through another hour of worship service, nary a snake in sight.

During Sunday school, some kid tells the teacher that one of their classmates has a Black dad and a White mom. The other kids all perk up, curious about this arrangement. The teacher recognizes this as a teaching moment. She quotes 2 Corinthians.

"The Bible says do not be unequally yoked," she tells us.

I don't know what "unequally yoked" means exactly, but I get the point: the Bible says having a Black dad and a White mom is bad.

My parents bring me a little notepad so I can at least entertain myself by drawing during an hour-long worship service that feels twice as long. The only sermon topics that get my attention: sex, violence, God's wrath, and hell.

Mostly, the preacher reads a Bible story and then rattles off non sequiturs that really drive home just how bad the world is getting *out there*, what with all the sexy prime-time television, satanic rock music, and gays crowding into Disney World. This particular Sunday morning, he celebrates his intellectual victory over an atheist he'd debated during his seminary years.

"The *fool* says in his heart, there is no God!" our preacher yells. "This fool, he challenged me, asking, 'Why is it that the Bible says in Revelation that there will be no sun in heaven?' And do you know what I told that sly ol' atheist? That the Word of God *also* says that God *himself* will provide all the light we need to see, to be warm, to grow gardens!"

An amen or two issues from the congregation. I make a face. Post-Armageddon, God will *literally* become the sun?

"And that ol' atheist, he was a clever one!" the preacher goes on. "He asked me, 'Well, Preacher, why is it that the Bible says that hell is a place of eternal fire and *also* a place of eternal darkness? Which one is it?' And you know what I said? I looked that ol' atheist right in his eye and I told him that the Word of God *also* says that the Lord is the light of the world! Without him, not even the flames of hell can provide light for the wicked!"

I squinted at my notepad. Wait, so Jesus is our source of *literal* light?

Sure. It says so in the Bible. Meanwhile, somewhere along a dirt road not far from where I was sitting, someone was having a rattlesnake worship party at church, and I was missing it.

THE ENDING OF MARK THAT ISN'T IN MARK

Here's a weird bit that shows up in some translations of the Gospel of Mark, chapter 16: "They will pick up snakes with their hands; and when they drink deadly poison, it will not hurt them at all; they will place their hands on sick people, and they will get well."

Thing is, this passage is widely accepted by Bible scholars as an *addition* to the original text. It's not in the earliest manuscripts, then at some point, it shows up in the copies. Someone was reproducing Mark's writing, and they thought to themselves, this is good, but it's not *snake-handling* good. They thought to themselves, the only thing missing is the part where we drink deadly poison.

So they added it in.

God didn't tell Mark to write it, so Mark didn't write it, but that didn't stop it from single-handedly spawning a small Appalachian movement of snake-handling churches and more than a dozen reported deaths from rattlesnake bites since the '40s, like no one thought to barrel into the Sunday snake worship party and shout, Hey! Hey! It's okay! This part isn't actually in the Bible!

And maybe the pastor, in wide-eyed disbelief, maybe he wouldn't believe them at first, but inside I bet he'd feel pretty relieved.

THREE FROG DEMONS

Many of the people who gave up on the Bible find in this dense, ancient volume a straw that breaks the back of their faith in Scripture. For me, it might have started with the three frog demons.

Other issues compounded over the years—the same issues that the Bible's readers have squabbled over for centuries, like slavery and genocide and that weird part where Elijah summons a bear to maul a bunch of children who mocked his baldness. There were other issues, but for me, it might have been the three frog demons that put the first real crack in the foundation, the first black blossom of mold in the walls.

In the fall of 1994, I sat down in my bedroom and opened my Bible. I was about to read the last book, Revelation, cover to cover. My youth pastor, he told me that Revelation was the only book in the Bible that promised a blessing just for reading it, and I wanted that blessing.

Sure enough, only three verses in: "Blessed is the one who reads aloud the words of this prophecy, and blessed are those who hear it and take to heart what is written in it, because the time is near."

I started over, reading aloud this time, just to be sure. The way I figured, if I read aloud, I say it *and* hear it. That's a double blessing.

My youth pastor, he reiterated what I'd always been told: The last book in the Bible is about the end of the world. The stuff in the book hasn't happened yet, but it will, and any day now. Really timely stuff.

So, I read it, and I liked it. It was bananas.

By chapter sixteen, I was lost in the tangled labyrinth of psychedelic visuals. Seven angels begin to dump "bowls of God's wrath" on earth, which bring down blood and darkness and festering sores. Suddenly, a dragon opens its mouth and out stroll three demons that "look like frogs." I finished the book, finding it equal parts entertaining, horrifying, and beautiful.

I looked out the window and realized it was night. *Saved by the Bell: The College Years* would be starting soon, but who knew if the world would last long enough to find out if Zack and Kelly would end up together?

Stacked on my VCR were a half dozen Godzilla movies on VHS, their tattered cardboard slipcases disintegrating from years of handling. I tried to imagine the demon frogs bounding out of the open jaws of a devil dragon, but all I could picture were the rubber suits and exploding miniatures of Japanese Kaiju movies. There was a terrible nagging sensation in my heart.

I found all of this very hard to believe.

No one told me, Hey kid, haven't you ever seen a political cartoon? One of those single panels populated by talking donkeys and elephants in patriotic top hats? It's not that the cartoon "isn't true," you just have to know what you're looking at is all. No one told me that it wasn't Revelation's fault that I didn't know how to read it.

Chapter 3

THE BRUTALITY OF FACT

FRANCIS BACON HELPS ME understand the Bible. Not the English philosopher with the funny hat, but the English painter whose work is the stuff of beautiful nightmares. Look at Bacon's *Three Studies for Figures at the Base of a Crucifixion* and you'll see what I mean.

A lot of Bacon's famous paintings feature screaming faces that seem to melt into black explosions, the misshapen visages of monstrous brutes, grotesque and eyeless creatures, that sort of thing. It's weird, then, that Bacon himself described his art as an effort to "trap reality," and that the art he prefers is the kind of art that possesses what he called "the brutality of fact."[1]

So, Francis Bacon painted a series of self-portraits. One of them ("Self-Portrait," 1969) captures the artist's face as a twisted mask of pink and purple bisected by bolts of bone white. His chin seems to split in two. One side of his crooked mouth snakes up the left side of his face like a Chelsea grin. Despite how deformed the thing is, Francis Bacon remains somehow recognizable in his self-portrait.

The brutality of fact.

Bacon painted himself this way on purpose and for a reason. It's not a put-on or a trick or a lie. His image is "deformed" by his artistic perception, interpreting the reality staring back at him from a mirror into the otherworldly profile rendered on canvas.

There are other ways to go about self-portraits. Some painters depict themselves with photorealism. Photographers and filmmakers do the same via different means. For the most part, we behold these images with respect for their mediums. You don't look at a photograph of a person, then at the actual person, and criticize a shadow that shows up in the photo but not in your immediate perspective. Nor should one scoff at Francis Bacon's warped purple head and say, "This is not what he *really* looks like."

These photos and films and paintings document and comment on true things about reality, but to understand what these true things are or how the images comment on them, you have to learn to understand and appreciate each visual in light of its medium, artist, and context.

In most of my many conversations with people who have become frustrated and disillusioned with the Bible, I end up feeling like we're talking about two very different books. Sure, not everyone who doesn't like the Bible is guilty of biblical illiteracy. There are plenty of people who, as best as they can, understand what the Bible is and isn't, and even then, they just don't like what it has to say. Like Bacon's inherently divisive self-portraits, the observer is invited to respond. Maybe you love it, maybe you hate it, or maybe you're not quite sure what the heck you're looking at.

DROWNING ANIMALS AND SEVERED HEADS

Listen. We're about to get into it. When I explain and defend what I think about the Bible, it probably won't sound much like how some other books explain and defend the Bible. I can tell you about those other books and I will.[2] But what good is it, me dragging up all the things I learned in grad school about ancient manuscripts and the Dead Sea Scrolls? I'm glad I learned that stuff, but someone already wrote those books, and this isn't one of them.

For me, the whole thing really began (and ended) with Jesus.

For all the imperfections of the Southern world that raised me, I grew up instilled with the smiling face of Jesus so that he became in my mind a loving, familiar friend. For all the terminal, gangrenous rot of American evangelicalism, its deep-seated tradition of Jesus as personal Savior seeped into my consciousness and wired the electric firing of my brain at the sight of his face, the mention of his name.

It hadn't always been great, this thing with Jesus and me. As with any relationship, there were patches of bad road. I often mistrusted Jesus, suspected him of malicious intent. I didn't always do what Jesus asked. Jesus would say, "I love you," and I would say, "Liar." Jesus would tell me his story, and I would doubt that it was true. Jesus promised to show me God, but God was mostly distant and threatening, and really, I was afraid of him.

My hang-ups were the same as everyone else's. Jesus, I don't understand these writings you're always on about. I don't like the world or the way you run it. I don't like the other people who claim to know and love and follow you.

If anyone asked, I'd tell them Jesus and I were getting along just fine. I could be real phony like that. I didn't want to be a sellout, so I'd usually say that Jesus and I were doing just fine, and a lot of the time, we were, but sometimes things weren't going well. I may not know much now, but I knew even less then, and I thought love was some seamless euphoria, an easy-breezy cosmic connection that mostly worked itself out, like rom-coms and soul mates, both of which are totally made up.

Sometimes I thought I wanted to be alone, but I couldn't seem to find whatever "alone" was—I couldn't escape the distant, singsong, whispering closeness of Jesus, like one of those bad poems you see inscribed on an oil painting in your grandma's bathroom. I'd read that one about the footprints in the sand, and I'd roll my eyes, but inside I was thinking, yeah, that's spot-on. Inside I was sniffling, a lump in my throat.

The biggest complication was that everything I knew about Jesus was in the Bible. Mostly, I liked the four biographies of Jesus—the Gospels—though even those books could be frustrating at times. It was the rest of the Bible I liked less. I'd been eyeing the whole thing with suspicion for as long as I could remember, grimacing at well-meaning Sunday school teachers as they pointed to flannelgraph images of Noah and his parade of smiling animals. They'd say, "And that's the story of the rainbow!" but I was imagining millions of screaming and struggling men, women, children, and animals as violent floodwaters engulfed them, the horror setting in that when God decides to kill you, that's that.

I was using a brown crayon to color little David's slingshot, but I was thinking about Goliath's severed head rotting in the sun as David dragged it back to Jerusalem. I was taught that it's not a good thing to saw someone's head off with a sword and drag it around as proof of your victory, but in the Bible, it was, apparently, a pretty great thing to do. In the Bible, it means that even when the odds seem bad (a little boy against a murderous giant), you too can decapitate adversity via the power of God.

INTERDIMENSIONAL SUPERBEINGS

Imagine a world in which the human civilization we know is a thing of the distant past. Imagine sophisticated superbeings of some far-flung future excavate the ancient ruins of Washington, DC, and Manhattan.

Two of these interdimensional travelers, students studying a world that once was, they pull from the fossilized remains of a fallen city fragments from a prehistoric image.

It's a photograph of George W. Bush standing beside Barack Obama. They recognize the species. Humans. They recall their teachers mentioning that Earth's archaeological record indicates that these particular humans were rulers of some kind. But what comes next is the discovery of a lifetime: a second parchment, this one almost perfectly intact.

It's a political cartoon.

In it, a caricature of Obama sits perched on planet Earth, pensive, reading a book about ISIS while the Middle East goes up in flames. In the second panel, a predictably cartoony George Bush wearing a holstered gun and cowboy boots desperately doctors the burning Middle East with a wrench and a missile, the ground scattered with screws and Band-Aids. Obama's panel is captioned "The Thinker," and Bush's, "The Tinkerer."[3]

The young superbeings feel as if incredible new light has been cast on the world of the past. Clearly, these particular humans possessed the ability to grow their forms to massive sizes in order to rule perched on the planet itself. (Their ears, for reasons yet unknown, became particularly huge during this process.) The superbeings can't read English, but a translation device suggests that the word on the left, "thinker," has to do with *thought*, and the word on the right, "tinkerer," has to do with *machines*. Thus, this reliable historical document clearly teaches that one of these gigantic planet-sized gods was the mind of Earth, and that he was empowered by the ancient Egyptian god, Isis, as the book in his hand indicates.

The second god must have maintained the mechanical functionality of the planet using enormous god tools and special god boots.

As these two students revel in the thrill of discovery, one of their teachers overhears them and approaches to see what all the fuss is about. Eyeing the document in question, the teacher scoffs.

"You dorks," the teacher says. "This image doesn't mean any of those things. That's not what it was for."

The students look at each other, confused. "Then what was it for?"

This is how people read the Bible. Like a bunch of clueless interdimensional superbeings misinterpreting a political cartoon. This is how you build churches on rattlesnake dances based on a passage that isn't even in the Bible in the first place.

The interdimensional students, embarrassed and frustrated, cast the political cartoon to the dust from whence it came. We were duped, they lament. This document isn't trustworthy at all! The entire expedition, they regret, has been a wash, and they return to their ship empty-handed.

66 MILLION (AND THREE) YEARS AFTER THE DINOSAUR APOCALYPSE

A herd of Tyrannosaurus rex probably saw a strange glowing shape in the sky above Hell Creek weeks before the age of reptiles came to a blazing hellfire conclusion.

I know this because I love dinosaurs.

In my earliest memory, I'm holding a tiny plastic Tyrannosaurus. It was 1985 or 1986, and I was clutching this shiny red dinosaur in the palm of my hand as my dad and my uncle carried my first "big boy bed" into my room. The T. rex wasn't paleontologically accurate. Its posture and shape and skin were all wrong. Now I know it was a mess, but at the time, it was pretty great.

I was a little kid learning the seven-syllable Greek names of dinosaurs like Pachycephalosaurus, and at my parents' insistence, rattling them off to doting grown-ups like a party trick. "Tell them what you want to be when you grow up," my parents would say, nudging whoever was obligated to listen, not wanting them to miss it.

"A paleontologist," I'd tell them. My parents would smile like, Did you hear that? How about *that*?

It was patronizing, but I didn't mind. I liked talking about dinosaurs. I would arrange dozens of plastic toys on the carpet of my room as I watched and rewatched a made-for-TV documentary, *Dinosaur!*, full of stop-motion puppets and narrated by Christopher Reeves, Superman himself. Talking to the camera, Mr. Reeves strolls through the American Museum of Natural History, musing as he pauses beside a Stegosaurus skeleton, "Join us now for this first-time-ever look at a world authentically recreated for this program—the world of the dinosaurs!"

I read a lot about what made the dinosaurs die out. Maybe a herd of Tyrannosaurus rex noticed a strange light in the sky, then suddenly, a flash.

The ground shook under their feet as if invisible forces were pulling a rug from beneath their heavy talons. Everything shot upward, came down, and went up again—a horrible playground game of parachute, snapping and splattering small animals on undulating terrain. Beads of burning glass and rock rained down on the prehistoric leviathans, shredding them like a hail of bullets, while, at the same time, the world itself became a broiling oven. The sky blackened with ash and soot, creating hurricane-force tornados shearing the surface of a cracked and burning world.

An asteroid the size of Mt. Everest, moving at speeds of 67,000 miles per hour, had hit Earth with the force of a billion atomic bombs. Then came nuclear winter and global warming to thoroughly kill most of the living things that managed to survive the first wave of the apocalypse.

Or, to hear my Sunday school teachers tell it, none of that happened.

My Sunday school teachers, they told me, "Just read the Bible. It's all right there. The whole process of going from no universe to an evolved cosmos featuring plants, animals, and human beings, the whole thing took 144 hours flat. Just read the first chapter. You'll see."

To hear my Sunday school teachers tell it, Adam and Eve rode naked on Tyrannosaurs, feeding them pomegranates and eucalyptus leaves. If you asked my Sunday school teachers about the crater in the Yucatán Peninsula—the spot where scientists believe the giant asteroid collided with Earth some 66 million years ago—my Sunday school teachers would say, impossible! The world, in all its biological complexity—they would say—was created in six 24-hour days. Read Genesis, they would say. It's right there on the first page.

Fossils? Well, maybe these generations of eggheads who dedicated their lives to books and universities and microscopes, who travel the world digging around for dinosaur bones, maybe they're all full of crap. Maybe they hate God.

66 MILLION (AND THIRTY) YEARS AFTER THE DINOSAUR APOCALYPSE

If you make really divisive art and enough people experience it, you'll find them in want of answers. I often write songs and stories when I'm upset. I didn't know this about God, that he did it too.

I wrote songs that told the truth about moments and feelings with images and characters both real and imagined. I mixed prose with hyperbole to tell stories and to document actual events and then paint them with wild visuals and metaphor. People would ask me, Why did you write this? Is this how you really feel? You wrote it down.

Yes and no. It depends on the type of writing and knowing how to read it. All of it tells the truth, some of it plainly. Other times, what's written is deliberately ambiguous, but the truth is in it, and if you can understand this, you can get to it a lot easier.

I thought I was a better, more complex artist than God. After all, I had been taught that God had penned a literal, linear, timeless ency-clopedia for life in the modern world. I didn't bother learning genre or style or tone or context because I didn't believe God had bothered with them either. Metaphor, I had been taught, means "not true." "Artistic" was just another way of saying "fictional." If the Bible was literary rather than literal, all was lost.

GOD'S BIBLICAL HATE

Nervous, practically shivering, I told a friend of mine, "I'm afraid that God hates me." Mostly, it was the Bible that bothered me.

A shambling bone heap of self-loathing and despair, I zeroed in on every angry, vengeful depiction of God in the Bible like a paleon-tologist looking for fossils. I would find these troubling passages and haul them up on my back, heavy burdens that bowed my spine and sent me lumbering deeper into my crisis of faith.

If there's any reason to suspect that God isn't fond of unfaithful screw-ups, then I'm in big trouble. It took six 24-hour days to create and complete the universe, and God hates the wicked. The Bible says both.

Later, I would read Bible scholars comparing the writing of Scripture to a multifaceted diamond, but at the time, I felt like I was carrying an ugly black stone that said one thing only. This is the Bible as I was taught to read it, more literal than literary.

Reeling and miserable, I thought maybe Adam and Eve did share celery stalks with Velociraptors, maybe there was no six-mile-wide dino-killing asteroid that hit Mexico, maybe there were just those six days because that's what the Bible says and it's time to come to grips with this: the Bible says God hates the wicked and that means you.

JESUS VS. ME VS. THE BIBLE

My favorite part of the Bible is in Matthew 5–7. It's usually called "The Sermon on the Mount," but really, it's Jesus's manifesto on what it means to follow him, to live well, to be human. This is the kind of thing Jesus called "The kingdom of God."

He says this near the beginning: "Do not think that I have come to abolish the Law or the Prophets . . ." (see Matt. 5:17–20).

Our Bible, the one with the pleather binding and gold-gilded tissue-thin pages, didn't exist when Jesus said these words. Jesus's "Bible" was what we now call the Old Testament, but first-century Jews referred to it as "the Scriptures," or "the Law and the Prophets."

Jesus says: "I have not come to abolish the Bible but to fulfill it."

The English word "abolish" has been translated from the Greek word *kataluō*.[4] It means "break, destroy, overthrow." Matthew uses this same word elsewhere to describe the destruction and dismantling of buildings and institutions.

It means: deconstruct.

In the first century, this was a technical term for *disobedience*. Jesus was a Jewish rabbi with a set of teachings and a lifestyle so unique and so provocative that he feels the need to clarify his intentions: I'm not here to disobey the Scriptures. I'm not deconstructing them. I'm fulfilling them.

Already, I can relate to Jesus, having to defend himself against accusations of not taking the Bible seriously because my reading of the text differs from the literalist world of my upbringing. Jesus has to relieve concerns that he intended to throw the whole thing out. Something in the teaching and lifestyle of Jesus made the Bible fundamentalists of his day worry that he was a troublemaker.

And Jesus opens his manifesto by brilliantly setting himself against both the literalists and the deconstructionists. Am I picking and choosing my own version of the Bible? No. Am I committing to a black-and-white, literal, letter-of-the-law slavish obedience to the text? Not that either.

> For truly I tell you, until heaven and earth disappear, not the smallest letter, not the least stroke of a pen, will by any means disappear from the Law until everything is accomplished. (Matt. 5:18)

Jesus loves hyperbole and wild imagery. When will the Scriptures be invalidated? When pigs fly. When will the Bible become irrelevant? When hell freezes over. Not a single iota will be lifted from these pages. Not one dot of an i. Not one cross of a t.

Not even the slightest hook on a letter is going anywhere.

None of it will pass away, Jesus says, "until everything is accomplished."

Accomplished. Fulfilled.

Then Jesus starts up with a series of juxtapositions. In the teaching rhythm, Jesus will begin by saying, "You have heard it said . . ." Then he'll quote the Scriptures (or pervasive religious teaching) before saying, "but *I* tell you . . ." (see Matt. 5–7).

The Bible says this, but *I* tell you . . .

You know, for someone promising not to deconstruct the Bible, Jesus sure sounds like a guy doing exactly that. There was a time when my misunderstanding of this text gave me hope. Me and Jesus against the ugly Old Testament, I thought.

Me and Jesus against the Bible.

66 MILLION (AND TWENTY-ONE) YEARS AFTER THE DINOSAUR APOCALYPSE

Something about the teaching of Jesus speaks to the deepest level of my soul, but I don't always like it. This is one reason I believe Jesus is telling the truth. I know myself well enough at this point to recognize that there are times when what I want to be true isn't always best for me or for anyone else. I've been around enough human beings to recognize this as a predicament universal to the species.

People say, "Follow your heart," but I'd rather they didn't.

The story of Jesus speaks to me because, in one scene, Jesus is lovingly blessing little kids, and in another, he's calling religious leaders a bunch of snakes. Jesus's paradigm for God is of a gracious, loving Father who kisses the faces of his sinful, rebellious children, but the seriousness with which he regards evil is so intense that he says it's better to gouge your own eye out than to objectify women. One thing makes me gush. The other makes me nervous. I'm suspicious of voices that only tell me what I want to hear.

Were it me, I might emphasize one thing, but not the other. I'd conceive of a God who is either never angry or never not angry. A soft, enabling God who doesn't care enough to stop me from destroying myself, or a God so appalled at my relentless failure that he can't bear to look at me without retching. But in Jesus, our soul-longings to be known and loved, for an end to evil and injustice are realized in the unfathomable beauty of truly self-sacrificial love.

And all of this is in the Bible.

I was thumbing through the Bible, frustrated with dietary laws and talking donkeys without any grasp of the kind of story I was reading or why. Out of the whole bizarre library, the one thing that really made any sense to me was Jesus, but getting rid of the rest of the Bible was a brutish, indelicate effort, and I kept losing Jesus in the process.

I remember seeing cereal boxes with Stegosaurs swinging their heavy, spiked tails at Tyrannosaurs and thinking, This is impossible. I'd point at it and say to anyone within earshot, Hey, the cereal box is wrong. The Stegosaurus died out some 20 million years prior to the T. rex. In fact, the gap between the Stegosaurus and the T. rex is smaller than the gap between the T. rex and *now*.

Or maybe I wouldn't say it because dinosaur talk of this variety made everyone feel itchy. Twenty million years? Does Josh believe in evolution? Does Josh not trust the Bible? Does Josh hate God? It wasn't the dinosaurs that were bothering me so much as all the *other* stuff. The dinosaur problem became a symbol of something bigger. I oscillated between disillusionment and desperation, the Bible becoming a furious steer and me the cowboy on its back, one hand in the air as if to say to the world: Look how long I can hang on! And everyone was watching, waiting.

It's not that I wanted to strip the Bible down to spare parts, to expunge every worrisome passage and bathe in the safe yellow glow of the warm Jesusy stories that patted me on the head and gave me a cookie. I wanted to understand the Bible as Jesus seemed to understand it. I wanted to find the good and gracious Father Jesus seemed to recognize on every page.

Part of me realized that if the road to becoming a boxing champion or kung fu master was replete with pain and discipline and sacrifice, then truly apprenticing with Jesus had to be all the more intense. I didn't really want an accommodating Christianity; I doubt anyone really does. When we sanitize the Bible, reducing it to mystic spiritual bedtime stories, our effort to create an inoffensive Christianity, ironically, creates a Jesus no one really cares about following. A figment of our own imagination. Like wrapping a tie around your waist and calling yourself a black belt. Really, we know it's a sham.

I was slowly learning to receive the Bible as a work of art. Good art, I knew, challenges the person receiving it. Asks something of them. Somehow, good art can comfort us while simultaneously making us uncomfortable. What if the Bible was the greatest work of art?

I have a bad habit of projecting my imperfections onto God. If I find myself loathsome and contemptible, I can't help but assume God does too. I'm convinced we all do this from time to time, but there is a flickering connection in the heart of humanity, forever burning a gentle flame that originated in the fire of God. We're made in God's image. We see evil and injustice in the world, and something in us says *This should not be.* We see peace and generosity and justice, and something in us says *Yes and amen.*

The enduring beauty and electric soul-shock of Jesus's teaching haunted me. I had become so crystallized in my cynicism that the tentacles of American evangelicalism became, in my mind, the sickbed propping up the awfulness of the entire world. The Bible, to my estimation, was complicit in the whole ugly affair, but I couldn't help seeing solutions in the teachings of Jesus, and these teachings were in the Bible—the Bible Jesus believed he was fulfilling.

It wasn't that I thought Jesus was the only person as clever as me. It was that his words were a dull ache in my heart. I wanted to become a nihilist, to believe that, ultimately, everything was truly meaningless, but Jesus recognized profound meaning in life. I wanted to allow the black leak of hate in my heart to fill the dried and emptied cisterns of my compassion, but Jesus taught that to love was the greatest thing of all. The world looked like a screeching ball of cats locked in a battle to the death, and Jesus's decree of nonviolence, though it ran upstream against all human inclination, was more beautiful than bombs or bullets, better than sociopolitical vitriol, more powerful than apathy or fatalism.

Really, I wanted Jesus, but he was carrying a Bible.

Jesus immersed himself in this ancient text for decades. It's not that he managed to find a way to make the Bible work for him. To hear Jesus tell it, his life and teaching were a fulfillment of the Bible's story—a story Jesus claimed was about him (see John 5:39–40). In his book about the Bible, Andrew Wilson wrote:

> Ultimately . . . our trust in the Bible stems from our trust in Jesus Christ; the man who is God, the King of the world, the crucified, risen and exalted rescuer. I don't trust in Jesus because I trust the Bible; I trust the Bible because I trust in Jesus. I love him, and I've decided to follow him, so if he talks and acts as if the Bible is trustworthy, authoritative, good, helpful, and powerful, I will too . . . even if some of my questions remain unanswered, or my answers remain unpopular.[5]

I guess it could have been the case that I knew a lot more about the Bible than a first-century Jewish rabbi who had dedicated his life to studying the Hebrew Scriptures of his people and ancestors, memorizing most, if not all, of it. Maybe Jesus was primitive and ignorant, and I saw all the holes everyone else had missed.

Or maybe there was just a better way to read it.

PLAYING IN TRAFFIC

The Bible is a story, and that story begins with Yahweh—the one and only Creator God—creating a beautiful place in which to design and root human beings, who are to partner with God in an ongoing collaborative effort to bring beauty and goodness out of the raw materials of a garden brimming with potential.

The people say, "No thanks," and the project descends into chaos. This happens on page three of the Bible.

If I were God, maybe I'd scrap the project then and there or at least assume unilateral control of it, but if you keep reading the Bible, you'll see that Yahweh refuses to give up on his big idea of a loving, freely chosen partnership with humanity.

As if working with small children or barnyard animals, God's beautiful vision of collaborative union is constantly snagged on the foolish, self-destructive disobedience of his beloved. God dirties his hands in the absurdity of humanity's death wish, erecting codes, restrictions, and sophisticated guidelines around his children just to keep them from playing in traffic, to instill in them a glimpse of how they might become uniquely his and thus demonstrate his loving goodness to the rest of the world.

But we don't feel like it. Not really.

So, God says, Look, if you won't live within my beautiful vision, let me spell it out for you. Then, in the book we call Exodus, Israel is given the *law*. The law itself is not the vision, it's a means of directing Israel back to the vision. This regulated enclosure is not what God, nor his children, had in mind. The ideal has been compromised by unfaithfulness, and as humanity persisted in her selfishness, we forgot the ideal, seeing only the fence on all sides. All of it belongs to the same story—the vision, the ideal, the disobedience, the law, all of it.

I have not come to abolish the law, but to fulfill it.

Jesus has no intention of deconstructing the Bible. He's fulfilling the Bible's story. Left to our own devices, we might read Jesus's teachings as if they were a bouquet of proverbs. "Hey, ever thought of this? And also, this? And while I'm on that subject, consider this. Oh, and on an unrelated note, here are my thoughts on some other thing."

But the Sermon on the Mount is not a buffet of loosely connected words to the wise. It is beautifully and provocatively unified in a specific, linear progression. This is why Jesus begins all of it by addressing the Scriptures. He is establishing the authority and context out of which the Sermon on the Mount proceeds. In Jesus's mind, his manifesto on the kingdom of God is not a new idea. It's where we've been headed since Genesis.

Jesus is explaining the Bible that will never pass away.

Jesus understands that what follows might appear upon first listen a radical reimagining of the Scriptures, so he says, Listen, before we get into it, you need to understand this is not me doing away with the Bible. This is me drawing you further in the direction to which the Bible was always leading.

"You have heard it said, . . . but *I* tell you . . ."

Across my many complicated years and battles with the Bible, I have learned that understanding what Jesus meant is how you defy the herd mentality of the legalists *and* the deconstructionists. The Bible is not to be strip-mined for rules by obsessive legalists, nor is it to be dismissed as a mystic fairy tale by progressive deconstructionists, its bones plucked for decontextualized self-help spirituality. How do you escape the kind of literalism that forces Adam onto the back of a vegetarian Tyrannosaurus? How do you avoid the equally nonsensical phenomenon of the Bible being "progressed" to death until what's left amounts to all the spiritual authority of a fortune cookie?

The answer to both extremes is *biblical literacy.*

Jesus understands a sort of reciprocal relationship with the way we handle the Bible and the way we experience the kingdom of God. It has to do with allowing the complicated beauty and gracious authority of the text to transform who you are so that you become someone who moves beyond knowing and obeying rules to someone who lives in the freedom and beauty of God's truth.

Of God's story.

Chapter 4

SHUT UP, GALILEO

Somewhere in the bramble-scattered deserts of Southern California, we found a tiger behind a gas station. My friend was beside me, smoking a cigarette as the scabby, miserable-looking jungle cat paced the pathetic dimensions of its iron enclosure. Blinking sand out of my eyes, I asked a hairy man in a sagging tank top why he had a Bengal tiger behind his gas station.

"People love her," the man said, watching the tiger do its sad laps.

We were three weeks into another tour. I felt horrible for this tiger and even worse about the unrealistic amount of work necessary to improve its situation. I tried to imagine the tiger being loaded into a crate for a short trip to a better life. Maybe at the San Diego Zoo.

"Had her five years now," the hairy man said. I screwed up my face imagining the five years. Some fifty feet in the distance, the rest of the band was refueling the van under a lavender sunset. Someone was poking at a pay phone. A Spanish version of Shakira's "Whenever, Wherever" crackled out of rusted outdoor speakers.

"Man," my friend said, taking a long drag from his cigarette. "Tigers are magnificent." He flicked the smoldering butt to the ground, grinding it into a black smudge beneath the toe of his Converse.

"Dude," I said, "litter."

"Don't matter," my friend said, blowing smoke out of his nose. He turned, saying, "This world's gonna pass away."

"What?" I asked.

"Bible says so," he called out, the shape of him shrinking against the beige horizon.

The tiger went on doing its laps.

TOO LONG; DIDN'T READ

I give a friend of mine a lot of grief about claiming to hate Terrence Malick's divisive film *The Tree of Life*. Really, my friend hates the first half hour of it. With a running time of more than three hours, he watched less than 17 percent of the movie. He says, "I hate that movie," and I correct him, "Well, you hate the first half hour of it, and really, you hate it without the rest of the movie to give it context. You haven't actually seen the movie."

We do this a lot, people.

Take English comedian Russell Brand, for example. I like Russell Brand. I remember when he invited two members of the tiny yet once-notorious Westboro Baptist Church to be guests on his talk show. The ridiculous and squirm-inducing interview was depressing and hilarious. Russell Brand—famously enthusiastic about mystic spirituality—argued that maybe the small cult of Westboro Baptist was misrepresenting Jesus, what with their infamous "God Hates Fags" sandwich boards and protesting at funerals and all.

Brand said: "I just feel from what I've read of Jesus and what I've had explained to me, that his main message was definitely tolerance and love and truth and beauty and acceptance."[1]

His audience applauded their approval.

I thought it was weird, the way Russell worded his argument. He admits he hasn't really read the teachings of Jesus, but that doesn't stop him from summarizing them by saying he *feels* like the main message was "definitely" tolerance and love and truth, yadda yadda

yadda. Russell Brand says he read bits of Jesus and had other pieces explained to him, and from those bits and pieces, he's arrived at a positive take on the whole thing.

On the other hand, my friend, the guy who watched the first half hour of *The Tree of Life*, he condemned the entire three-hour film. Neither one is exactly what we'd call an informed position.

You don't have to be a scholar or a historian to have feelings about Jesus and the Bible, but when they significantly inform your life trajectory—for better or for worse—they might be worth a closer look.

BEST WORST BOOK

Whatever you think about the Bible, people who really want to read the thing are out there. Go online and watch footage of Chinese Christians receiving their own personal Bibles for the first time and you'll see them scrambling for their copies as if they're worried the books might vanish, like this is all a dream and they'll wake up. They clutch the Bibles to their chests, weeping, kissing the binding, pressing it to their faces as if it were a long-lost loved one.

Me? I find Bibles in my church lost and found every week. I see Bibles piled high in Goodwill donation bins. I was at a rock concert once where I saw what I can only assume was a very cheap copy of the Bible torn apart and set ablaze. The flaming book was tossed stage left, where a diligent stagehand rushed forward to douse it in the billowing white fog of a fire extinguisher, which sort of diminished the dramatic effect they must have been going for. Many years later, I found a YouTube clip of that moment. One commenter pleaded: "PLS RESPECT BIBLL!!!"

Entire books, lectures, podcasts, and careers have been dedicated to discrediting and debunking the Bible. The Bible has been cited as the motivation and justification for racism, sexism, violence, slavery, oppression, and war.

It's not exactly a mystery why the Bible has such a bizarre and polarizing effect on the world. Like any great work of art, the Bible is often misunderstood. Open the Bible, and you might find something overtly beautiful and inspiring without even trying. Or you could find something dark and unsettling just as easy. For all the blame placed on the Bible for making such a stink in the world, it can't be denied that this book has also shaped entire cultures for the better, spawning hospitals, orphanages, food banks, homeless shelters, and social justice.

Martin Luther King Jr. said that living and preaching the story of the Bible was his "first calling" and "greatest commitment." He said:

> "All that I do in civil rights I do because I consider it a part of my ministry. I have no other ambitions in life but to achieve excellence in the Christian ministry. I don't plan to run for any political office. I don't plan to do anything but remain a preacher."[2]

Even a lot of people who hate the Bible are probably grateful for Dr. King's civil rights movement that he himself attributed to the Bible.

The Bible is the most widely sold and circulated book that few people actually read. The Guinness Book of World Records argues that "although it is impossible to obtain exact figures, there is little doubt that the Bible is the world's best-selling and most widely distributed book."[3]

Despite its reputation as beloved amongst prudes and rule-mongers, the Bible is peppered with intense language, violence, explicit sex poems, adultery, betrayal, deception, incest, nihilism, orgies, dismemberment, rape, genocide, war, and murder. Some of it literal, some of it figurative. Some of it redemptive, some of it somber and bleak. Some of the crazy stuff is abstract or metaphoric, intended to teach and provoke. Some of the crazy stuff just records history. Some of it continues to defy easy explanation.

Like any great work of art, the Bible evokes reactions that range from adoration, to confusion, to anger, to defensiveness, to belligerence, to dismissal. The Bible and the people who love it become such a problem in the minds of a furious public that an effort was launched to somehow pry Jesus of Nazareth from the cold dead pages of this antiquated text.

We like Jesus, they say, but not the Bible. We like Jesus, they say, but not the church. It's like saying, We like Indiana Jones, but not Indiana Jones movies.

Fine, I guess. But how else do we know Indiana Jones but from Indiana Jones movies?

And really, who *doesn't* like Jesus? He advocated for the poor and the oppressed, empowered women, cared for the sick, embraced a lifestyle of simplicity. He spoke truth to religious hypocrisy and political power. There are enough great pull quotes from Jesus that you can create a lopsided caricature of the man to suit your preferences, and many people do exactly that.

"The truth shall set you free." That's Jesus.

"Don't cast your pearls before swine." Another Jesus original.

"Do to others what you would have them do to you." That's Jesus's unique subversion of an ancient axiom.

The funny thing is that even if you dispense with the Old Testament, you'd still have some of the Bible's most intense content in the four biographies of Jesus's life. Judgment, hell, the devil, excommunication, sexual ethics, money, nonviolence, state sedition; it's all there in the teachings of Jesus.

And at any rate, the effort to somehow pry the greater library of writings we call the Scriptures away from the biographies of Jesus (what we call the Gospels) never seems to work, because Jesus constantly appeals to the rest of the Bible as authoritative and indispensable. Jesus goes as far as to argue that the rest of the Bible is what lends credibility and context to his life and teaching.

So, it makes perfect sense that in the vast majority of cases, the struggle of frustrated, teetering Christians (usually those of us raised in conservative or fundamentalist environments) to diminish the Bible eventually results in the inevitable diminishing of Jesus himself. We come at the Bible with power tools, wanting to save Jesus, attempting delicate surgery with a chain saw.

HOW TO PRESERVE THE WORLD'S
MOST DANGEROUS BOOK

Pay tens of thousands of dollars for seminary, spend years reading all kinds of books about history and theology, ancient Greek and Hebrew, and here's some of what you'll learn.

It took many centuries to write the Bible, which isn't a book, but a library of books. Putting and keeping it together was complicated. At the end of the day, the whole thing has a very traceable—very *human*—origin, and that freaks people out. It freaks people out because the Bible, we've been told, is *God's* book.

But the Bible is completely unembarrassed about its complicated origins. It doesn't pretend to have been inscribed by God's laser. The Bible is like a wonderful eccentric. A lovable but baffling intellectual who invites you into their home, books crowded on every surface, papers stacked up and spilling onto the floor, and the eccentric is saying, "Come on in! Don't mind the mess!" Maybe you're mortified by the whole scene, but they have no idea they should be embarrassed at all.

The Bible will start books with things like, "The words of Jeremiah . . ." and you, the reader, you're thinking, "So who is the one *writing* 'the words of Jeremiah'?" Or maybe you'll get to the end of a book you thought was authored by Moses, but then Moses dies in that book and the story keeps going. Did someone else take over? Who? The Bible doesn't bother saying.

In Jeremiah 36, the prophet's scroll is set on fire and the whole thing has to be written all over again, but verse 32 says that as the scribe dictated Jeremiah's words, "many similar words were added to them." What words? From whom? Are the words we're reading some of those "many similar words"? I would think this is the kind of stuff we need to know, but the Bible isn't prissy about this sort of thing. The Bible cares less about its own clarity than legions of Bible legalists.

If you go digging around in antiquity, you'll learn that we don't have the original manuscripts of the biblical texts. We have copies. Lots of them. We have copies of the Hebrew Bible from AD 1008, and we have Greek translations of the Hebrew Bible that are even older, from sometime around 200 BC, and we have a cave full of thousands of Dead Sea Scrolls that are older still, from around 400 BC. We have so many copies—copies that many scholars and historians and linguists have pored over for decades—that we know about tiny discrepancies from one copy to the next. We know which versions circulated in certain regions and eras, and we know what kinds of footnotes ancient scribes left for future scribes whom they believed would make more copies.

Point is, we not only have all this to go on, but we also have the amalgamated wisdom and learning of experts from all over the world who have dedicated their lives to studying the Bible.

When it comes to Bible scandals, it seems that pop culture, Dan Brown, and Oprah have overpromised and underdelivered. If there are secret societies that exist to hide "lost gospels," they really suck at it. The stuff that isn't in the Bible you can buy at your local bookstore—like the truly bonkers *Gospel of Thomas,* in which Jesus promises to perform a supernatural gender reassignment on Mary Magdalene. This and other works aren't in the Bible because we have mountains of writings spread out across thousands of years, and the Bible has mostly retained its basic shape, give or take a few well-known squabbles across certain traditions. There was no giant conference room held up by marble pillars where bearded elites—motivated by power, position, and political agenda—pulled an all-nighter, putting the Bible together once and for all. Go pick up a copy today, and what you'll read is what Christians around the world have been reading for centuries. Like it or not.

Really, the Bible strikes us as strange because the way it was written and transmitted is so unlike the way modern people tend to think a credible historical document comes into being. A few decades probably passed between the events of the Gospels and the moment when someone finally sat down to commit the story to papyrus. In that gap, the story thrived via oral tradition—it was shared aloud by people whom Luke described as "eyewitnesses and servants of the word" (Luke 1:2), people who saw everything happen firsthand, and other officially sanctioned and trustworthy storytellers who were responsible for preserving and relaying the story accurately amongst elders, families, and communities.

Eventually, those stories were written down. Scribes and copyists replicated the manuscripts, which circulated with the planting of churches as the Jesus movement proliferated throughout the ancient Mediterranean.

Really, the manuscript histories of the Old and New Testaments are extensive and well recorded. The Bible may be very old, but we know what's in it, and every year we learn more about how it was meant to be read.

But there are two ways of understanding how the Bible *really* came to be in the first place. On the left, we have the theologically liberal, or "progressive," if you like, which maybe grants that the Bible is a work of ancient literature with the odd nugget of wisdom, but does not believe it is "authoritative Scripture."

For them, the Bible is a very human library and little more. Depending on who you ask, maybe these human authors did enjoy some encounter with "god" (whatever *that* means), and maybe they wrote about it, but God himself wasn't in the office when they cranked out the manuscripts. If you get rid of God as a direct player in the Bible's writing, construction, and transmission, then you're left with an ancient and thus painfully outdated take-it-or-leave-it collection of writings of some historical significance, but that may or may not intersect with our world in any meaningful way. Like Homer's *Iliad* or Tolkien's beloved sleeping pill, *The Lord of the Rings*.

This is how you get a very palatable Bible if you want it. This ancient library may have some upsetting things in it, but it is, after all, just another ancient book by primitive peoples. Why bother applying the fine details of this antiquated text to life in the here and now? Look at it, instead, like Aesop's Fables or *The Cat in the Hat*.

This is how you create a pop radio Bible. A Bible that never challenges or offends because it doesn't have its anachronistic hands in your life. If you go looking for Jesus this way, chances are you'll emerge with a figure of your own design. An inspirational space

Gandhi. He likes what you like. He's irked by what irks you. His causes are your causes, and you quote him accordingly. If you feel you are being judged, call on Jesus, because didn't he say something about not judging?

In your mind, no one gets Jesus right, least of all Christians. Your Jesus never bothers you at all. He's convenient. He's comfortable. He doesn't really ask you to do anything you don't want to do.

But really, what's the point? If we're doing arbitrary surgery on the Bible, using some imaginary rubric to assign value to some things and delete others, doesn't it make the most sense to just drop the whole thing altogether? If the Bible is entirely wrong about significant things—like, say, that Jesus is the only truth, the only way to God—then any "wisdom" the Bible has to offer is questionable at best. It's like going to Jeffrey Dahmer for relationship advice.

"I don't agree with *everything* he says, but that Dahmer made some great points."

The Bible as a flawed, human, but occasionally helpful volume of Aesop's Fables doesn't make much sense.

But if you move from the left all the way to the rightmost side of the spectrum, you get something called Biblicism, or the *idolatry* of the Bible. Here, the Bible is entirely understood as authoritative Scripture with absolutely no regard whatsoever for the Bible as art or literature. Consequently, the Bible becomes something like a Mormon artifact that fell from heaven on golden tablets.

Understanding the Bible as a crystal clear telegram from God never works because everyone who reads it must enter into the process of *interpretation*. Most of the Bible's modern readers aren't fluent in ancient Greek or Hebrew, so we rely on other people to translate the text before we even get to it. None of us lived in the ancient world of the Bible, and a lot of us don't know much about it. It's not like the Bible's authors said to themselves, Wait, I better explain this in such a way that the people of the future reading it in a yet-to-be-invented language on glowing glass slabs will understand it as they glide down highways on their hoverboards. The world of the Bible often sounds as bizarre to us as our world would have sounded to the Bible's authors thousands of years ago.

Maybe if you were God, you'd have seen to the writing of a helpful and timeless volume void of symbolism or poems or parables. Something that translates immediately across time and space. A book where "six days" always means six literal 24-hour days and loping demon frogs are just demon frogs and anyone who can't deal with it is just a godless heathen because it is what it is so get over it.

But that isn't the Bible. And for centuries, students of the Bible have devoted themselves to the meticulous study of this infinitely complex feat of divine/human literary art.

Anyone who reads the Bible brings lenses with them—their own culture, their own context, their own stories and backgrounds and bents. We are, after all, human. That's not at all bad, because the Bible was authored by humans who did the same thing. Understanding the Bible as itself divine eliminates the human element of its authorship, which makes understanding a book written and read by humans nigh impossible.

Disciples of Jesus down throughout history have held that the Bible's authors were inspired by God's Spirit—that in some strange, divine process, these human authors wrote what *they* wanted to write, empowered and inspired by God himself. In their writing, God's Spirit "breathed out" what *God* wanted to say. Christians have never held that the Spirit put these authors into a helpless trance, possessing and puppeteering them as their pens moved independently of their brains. Instead, the personalities, aesthetics, agendas, cultures, contexts, moods, and quirks of the human authors are right there on the page, and the Bible is more interesting for it.

This becomes a tremendous complication when one attempts to read the Bible as an entirely literal, linear, timeless, one-size-fits-all manual for life in the modern world. J. I. Packer described the disposition with which he approaches the Bible as "an advance commitment to receive as truth from God all that Scripture is found on inspection actually to teach."[4]

That, for me, is the balance in a nutshell.

The left does not receive the Scriptures as truth from God. The right doesn't enter into the complicated work of inspecting the Scriptures to discover what they actually teach. Mystery, for human beings, is uncomfortable. Mystery takes time. Ancient students of the Scriptures took this for granted, that the Bible gives up more of its riches across a lifetime of meditation, but we are the people of Amazon Prime. We like our mysteries resolved with ruthless efficiency. A book that is somehow both human and divine is mysterious, and we'd prefer it be one or the other. Jesus, on the other hand, accepted this mystic dichotomy as a given.

In Matthew 22, Jesus quotes a poem written by King David. The story goes:

> He said to them, "How is it then that David, speaking by the Spirit, calls him 'Lord'? For he says, "The Lord said to my Lord: 'Sit at my right hand until I put your enemies under your feet.'" (vv. 43–44)

Jesus describes the poem's authorship as "David, speaking by the Spirit." In one small phrase, Jesus encapsulates a dense theology of how the Bible works. It's *David* talking—there's a very human author. But the human author is speaking *by the Spirit*. Jesus is appealing to the voice of *God* through the voice of *David* through the voice of *Scripture*.

Characteristically profound, Jesus reveals with a passing phrase that for him, the Scriptures are more than just the product of human imagination—that would have been "David speaking" and nothing more. But neither does Jesus understand the Scriptures as some kind of divine dictation void of any human component. It's David doing the speaking, but he's doing it *by the Spirit*. Jesus understands the sacred Hebrew Scriptures as a collaboration between one divine author and other human authors. But many of the Bible's readers desperately want it to be only one of those two things.

THE MUSICIANS ARE REVOLTING!

Imagine a room full of musicians. Imagine that in this room of musicians, there are a few who are classically trained and educated in music theory. They are talented, capable, and they know their stuff. But also in this room are some musicians who, while talented and capable, are untrained, can't read music, don't know theory. More of a DIY, self-taught kind of thing.

Imagine that in this room full of musicians, a conflict arises.

One of the untrained musicians is looking down at a piece of music he can't read, and he says, "You know what, man? I'm having some trouble with this."

Another musician asks, "What? Trouble with what?"

"*This*," the first musician says, gesturing at the whole room. "All of *this*. It's like, how do we even know that this stuff on this paper is really *music*, know what I mean?"

And another one pipes up. "You know, I've been thinking *the exact same thing*. Could be anything on there. And look at this part!"

This other musician points at a complex knot of notes on the page. "What is this part?" he asks the room. "I don't like the look of this at all."

A little rabble is forming. Someone raises the stakes. "Listen, I've got to be honest, I have never liked drums. They hurt my ears. It's insensitive. A lot of hearing loss has been done by drums. They just seem so outdated and unnecessary. Who says we have to pound on these primitive things to be drummers, anyway?"

That seems weird, but the others, enjoying the comradery, decide to go with it. "Dang, they've got a point. Drums *are* pretty loud!" At this point, the disturbance is such that other musicians, the ones who know theory and have been in the game their whole lives, take notice.

"What's all this about drums and sheet music?"

So, the dissenters, they start to vocalize their beef with everything. What's even on this paper? Why should this sheet of paper tell us how to play this song? And has anyone noticed how insensitive drums are?

At first, the more experienced musicians are pretty gracious about it. Well, *you* may not be able to read the music, but trust us, that's music. We didn't make it up. Many people have dedicated their lives to the reading and writing of it. It's not nonsense if you know how to read it. And yes, drums can hurt your ears, but there's not necessarily a problem with the entire concept of drums.

But this only further frustrates the young musicians. Here we go with this backward, antiquated music legalism! The disillusioned musicians start to form alliances. One of them writes a book: *Leaving Sheet Music Behind: My Brave Journey from Fundamentalism to Freedom*. It becomes an international best seller peering out from endcaps on Target aisles. Their social media platform is bolstered. Other frustrated and untrained musicians go to them for advice. Their answers are faster and easier than learning to read sheet music.

The trained musicians, they're pleading with these frustrated young players. "Well," they reason, "sheet music itself is not really fundamentalism. That's not what that word means."

Now the music deconstructionists are furious. They start a podcast and invite victims of drum volume violence to share their survival stories in a safe space. They say things like, For me, personally, my truth is that actual musical notes don't exist so much as *feelings* about truth and love. It's the energy of the universe. It's everything. Like, the chair I'm sitting in could be a musical note, y'know!

"Wow," the cohost says. "Wow, you are so blowing my mind right now."

This profound insight becomes immortalized in the undeniable legitimacy of a hashtag. #mychairisamusicalnote sweeps social media outlets, collecting new deconstructionists. Parents cry; followers and ad revenue soar!

Some of the other musicians are caught in the middle of the whole thing. They were learning to read music but are becoming increasingly frustrated with the challenge of mastering an instrument. The time it takes. The discipline and self-sacrifice required. They start to ask themselves things like, "Why should I have to sacrifice part of myself to learn this instrument?" They start to wonder, "Is this toxic?" Books are too slow, so they take to social media for answers. They find the deconstructionists and think, Dang, maybe these other guys are on to something. Their way sure sounds a whole heck of a lot easier, anyway.

The trained musicians are stuck in the past. Baffled and discouraged, they can only say, "Listen, your chair is not a musical note."

THE ANSWER TO BIBLICAL DISILLUSIONMENT: BIBLICAL LITERACY

People have issues with the Bible. Some of said issues are, dare I say, justified. Many awful things have been said and done in the name of the Bible. But what also tends to upset people is the unavoidable reality that the Bible has a lot to say about what is good and what is evil and how people should live as a result. People, as a general rule, don't like to be told what is good and what is evil, or how they should live, apart from their own preferences and fragile sensibilities.

The Bible comments on science, politics, and life in the modern world, and the Bible intends to impact the way we think and live, but the Bible's preferred means of doing this isn't with copy/paste dos and don'ts, but by *forming* us slowly over time as we sit in deep contemplation of a beautiful and mysterious story.

The Bible describes itself as a work intended for ongoing consideration.

> Blessed is the one
>   who does not walk in step with the wicked
>
> or stand in the way that sinners take
>   or sit in the company of mockers,
>
> but whose delight is in the law of the Lord,

and who meditates on his law day and night.
(Psalm 1:1–2)

How fortunate, the poem goes, how *blessed* is the one who delights in the Bible! Who loves the Bible! How blessed is the one who meditates on what it says. You hear the word "meditation," and you think yoga. You think sitting silently, emptying the mind. But the Bible describes a focused reader who intends to *fill* their thinking and feeling with the profound truth woven into the Bible's beautiful and complex story.

Which explains a lot. Like many great feats of artistry, the Bible refuses to give up all its wonder and majesty with a simple, superficial reading. The reader must learn to move backward and forward through the text, uncovering more of the unified whole woven into seemingly disconnected stories, unanswered questions, and troubling passages.

And in this lifelong endeavor, you are unearthing new insight into a staggering literary achievement, a beautiful and provocative work of art that combines narrative, poetry, and discourse uniquely crafted to be read and reread over a lifetime, giving up new dimensions of wisdom and truth with each new journey across its many pages.

It's almost as if God himself was the coauthor.

Thus, the Bible describes its ideal reader in Psalm 1 as someone who delights in the story and who meditates on it day and night. For years I felt as if I was missing something with the Bible because I couldn't bring myself to love it the way I loved other things that entertained me. I felt a distant pang of guilt that, in my heart of hearts, just about everything else was more interesting than the Bible of my upbringing.

My youth pastor scolded me and my friends when he learned that we'd watched an outrageous tour documentary of the band Pantera that was making its way through certain members of the youth group like some black-market VHS bootleg. The youth pastor was predictably bummed that we'd entertained these video antics of sex, drugs, and rock and roll, and he asked me through a scowl, "Did you read your Bible that day?"

I hadn't.

"So, you gave up time with God to enjoy time with Satan," the youth pastor concluded.

Is that what I had done? I didn't want it to be true, and I doubt I would have admitted it to anyone (least of all myself), but the idea of watching that Pantera VHS felt dangerous and interesting, the promise of madness and music, a voyeur's window into a kind of depravity that repulsed rather than titillated.

I didn't know how to delight in the Bible because I was given no paradigm for the Bible's aesthetic. If I really loved God, I thought, I'd want to read his book, learn all the rules, and behave accordingly. I assumed that the average work of art and my reaction to it was more complex and dynamic than my relationship with the Bible, a moral encyclopedia for life.

I knew what it meant to love a work of art that I didn't fully understand. Or to love a work of art that also bothered me. I knew what it meant to have my incomplete understanding of, or discomfort with, a work of art be among my greatest reasons for loving it. But I hadn't learned how to read the Bible.

The Bible is so profoundly complex, but we think appreciating it is simple.

And we get frustrated.

Because the Bible won't do what we want it to do. The Bible refuses to explicitly answer modern science questions, so Bill Nye has to go on TV to debate with a guy who built a whole museum to argue that a few thousand years ago people were riding around on vegetarian Tyrannosaurs.

The Bible fundamentalists go around with their broken record mantra: "The Bible *clearly* says . . ." Which is hilarious because if that were true, we wouldn't have hundreds of splintering denominations and movements and thousands of debates and books and people like me aggravating someone reading this book because I inferred in the last paragraph that people *didn't* ride on vegetarian Tyrannosaurs.

I'm sorry. Believe me, I wish it were true. No one wishes it more than me.

We get frustrated with the Bible when we try to make it do what it isn't meant to do. The Bible can be frustrating—I believe there are times when it intends to be—but I think most of our frustration comes from us wanting to go fast when the Bible wants to go very slow. The Bible is designed as the kind of literature one reads, day and night, for a lifetime without exhausting the layered riches within.

And that's meant to excite us rather than dissuade us. That's the Bible's idea of encouragement. "Relax, it'll take a lifetime."

Success, for a reader of the Bible, isn't referencing random texts for life lessons, like an encyclopedia, but in moving backward and forward, long bouts and short sessions, slowly and carefully, with ongoing consideration and new insights as we grow and are shaped by the text itself.

You are meant to grow in competency and confidence as you read and learn, but you don't crack the code for a literal and linear manual for life in the modern world—you understand that as you are formed, you will continue to uncover new riches in the bottomless depths of wisdom and artistry that the Scriptures have to offer. And in all the beauty and strangeness and wrestling of the reader with the text—the reader with God—you learn what it means to delight in this work of art.

We delight in even the ambiguity of the Scriptures because it is an invitation to go deeper, to wrestle, to know more, to meet God himself in the text. This work of art is not subjective. It is not meant to inspire unique translations from different readers but to bring every reader into the same, unified story of God.

And we need other students of the story for that.

THE COMMUNITY RULE

Among the ancient Jewish manuscripts that came to be known famously as the Dead Sea Scrolls, one such document was first known as the *Manual of Discipline* before it was later designated, *Community Rule*. In it, an ancient Jewish community refers to the Bible as "the scroll of meditation," using the same word from Psalm 1. For centuries upon centuries—for *thousands* of years—those who delight in the Bible, who meditate on it day and night, have also understood that the complex beauty of this library is simply too extraordinary to house in one lonesome brain.

Reading the Bible requires entire communities of men and women, young and old, dedicated to God's authority vested in the text and to pondering what it says and working out what it means together— never in isolation.

There's a kind of theory and science to the whole thing. Doctors have "the medical community." If someone within the community comes along suddenly arguing, Hey, I've discovered the cure for the common cold, the rest of the community will appropriately respond by asking: What is it? Show us your research. Let us read and test it. Let us see how it harmonizes or deviates from the research of others who have come before you. If the purported cold-curing miracle turns out to be Windex, and if the one claiming the discovery scorns existing science and research, and if Windex doesn't cure the common cold, then the claim is rejected as false. Even if someone really, really wants Windex to cure the common cold.

Like any endeavor involving human beings, error and corruption can and do creep into this process from time to time. The community rule isn't perfect, but it is necessary and crucial. The community rule honors the wisdom and work of the medical tradition. When it works best, it opens itself to entertain and evaluate new ideas that might deviate from tradition but ultimately provide a better understanding and practice of medicine—but not before they are tested.

This is exactly how the church applies the community rule to understanding the Scriptures. This is how we establish and maintain orthodoxy. It isn't perfect, but it is necessary and crucial, bringing the minds of countless men and women from all over the world with innumerable backgrounds across centuries to bear on how we understand what the Bible intends to teach. This diverse collective mind becomes an ongoing effort to guard against misinterpretation, false teaching, and abuse.

If and when someone comes along with a new reading of the Bible— a reading that steps beyond that rich, diverse, ancient tradition—it must be tested by the community. New readings are accepted into the open-mindedness of orthodoxy if they harmonize with the whole of Scripture, with our sincere theological effort to understand it, and with the community that belongs to the Jesus tradition. Ideas that deviate from all three are rejected as heresy. This way, no one person is responsible for the profundity of the Bible.

That's a lot better than trying to figure it out all on your own.

Sometimes, we really want Windex to cure the common cold, even though centuries of study from people all over the world confirms that it does not. Frustrated and hurt, we go looking for someone, anyone, who will tell us that Windex does cure the common cold. With enough looking, you can find such a person. Several people. You can build a little movement around it. Modern, affluent American people love to do this—to shake our superior heads at those poor and oppressed people of color around the world who wrote the Bible and died to preserve its teaching.

Sorry, you sad, deluded barbarians. A few Americans have moved on. Get with the times!

SHUT UP, GALILEO

Bible disillusionment and deconstruction are all the rage right now. Very hip. Very marketable. They sell books, generate podcast subscribers, and drive up brand revenue with the promise of intellectual rebellion against the religious establishment. Never mind the rich history of centuries' worth of doctors, philosophers, astronomers, scientists, physicists, mathematicians, historians, and theologians who followed the historic Bible-informed way of Jesus. We've moved past that.

Ignorance is a powerful tool. Professor Tom Nichols worries that "Americans have reached the point where ignorance . . . is an actual virtue. To reject the advice of experts is to assert autonomy, a way for Americans to insulate their increasingly fragile egos from ever being told they're wrong about anything."[5]

Who needs Galileo, C. S. Lewis, Mother Teresa, Martin Luther King Jr., Dorothy Day, George Washington Carver, or N. T. Wright, when you've got everything's-okay, you're-good, it's-all-about-your-happiness, love-more-suffer-less books? Maybe there was a time when those old academics, intellectuals, and humanitarians might have lent a certain credibility to Bible lovers, but now we know they were all duped. We're smarter than they were.

If only they had seen this one YouTube video. If only they had heard this one podcast.

Sure, some of these historic figures faced down the evils of the world head-on, cared for the sick and oppressed without denouncing the way of Jesus. Sure, some of these historic figures dedicated their lives to studying and learning, decades upon decades given to loving God with the mind for the sake of future generations of the church, and they continued to live under the unapologetic lordship of Jesus.

But these new guys have a podcast!

Who needs PhDs and decades of faithful discipleship and pastoral experience around the world when you have Instagram and Twitter? The Bible is bad news.

For starters, the Bible is always on about inherent human evil, as if our primitive base desire could ever be wrong. If there's one thing our fragile popular culture has taught us, it's that anyone or anything that asks you to deny your own desire and intuition is wrong. Not to be trusted. Dangerous.

The irony is, of course, that we let outside sources change our minds all the time. An article, a documentary, a podcast. We're actually suckers, humans. We just think of ourselves as enlightened because we trust one thing and not another.

Everyone chooses a master.

I get it. Christians are not the only good or smart people in the world. You can also make a list of very intelligent, impressive, influential non-Christians and atheists. (I read, appreciate, and learn from a lot of them.) And no, not every Christian is a great example. You can also make a damning list of alleged Christians who have believed and accomplished very unintelligent and destructive things.

But who is teaching us? From whom do we seek out answers? How do we balance them?

Are we basing our spiritual journey on the accumulated wisdom of centuries worth of thinkers who dedicated their lives to the slow process of discipleship, learning to be wrong, worked out in the accountability of community? Or are we throwing out a two-thousand-year-old movement based on the gripes of a few twenty-somethings who are mad at their parents? Are a few months or even a couple of years with hurt feelings and jaded podcasters really our best resources for resolving ancient mysteries to which sages and saints have given their entire lives?

We've been trained like lab rats to devour and digest what the Information Age calls "content." We approach packets of content for the sweet, sweet information inside, tear it open, gobbling it up in an explosion of crumbs and debris like Cookie Monster, then move along, solidified in a new thing we now believe.

Self-help, politics, journalism, diet, media. You read the book or watch the YouTube video or binge the docuseries or skim the article or deep dive the conspiracy theory, and now you're all about Zen or minimalism or keto. You call this "doing the research." You're totally convinced that someone was a murderer, that there was a cover-up, that we should all eat this one thing and never eat this other thing ever again. You can't believe that no one realizes how important it is to breathe through your nose.

The idea is that information affords us more control over our lives. And we want control.

So, the Bible, that's dumb, ancient. No thanks. But a well-made Net-flix documentary? Sold. An op-ed in a publication that adheres to my political leaning? Crucial. Wild rants on an Instagram story? Fire. Everyone *needs* to read this. Hands raised emoji. #findyourtruth. #dowhatmakesyouhappy. My truth is that my chair is a musical note. If it's true for me, who's to say otherwise? Coexist.

You can go on about how all worldviews are equal and good, but every worldview claims truth against everyone else's lies, and every-one has a worldview. They contradict. They invite adherents into radically different ways of thinking and living. They all assume that there is actual moral knowledge. Not just an opinion or arbitrary belief, but that there are true and knowable things about meaning and existence.

The Hebrew writers call it *chokmah*, which we translate as "wisdom." It's not just decent advice. It's how one lives in rhythm with what is actually true and good. One way the Bible's worldview differs radi-cally from the Diet Coke, Instagram "you do you" ideology is that the Bible understands that in the same way that there are natural laws in the universe (gravity, thermodynamics, that kind of thing) there are also moral laws, relational laws, theological laws. This could be one reason why the Bible's particular approach to authority confuses so many readers. Because the Bible *does* have commands (lots of them, actually), and some of them aren't even for the reader, but for certain characters at a certain point in the story.

Sometimes we feel strongly that the Bible *should* have a command, and it doesn't. It just sort of reports information about something horrible without explicitly commanding the reader, Hey, don't try this at home. It's a bit like the confusion people often bring to satire: How can a very violent story actually intend to condemn violence? By telling a story that communicates what is true on that story's terms.

The Bible is an authoritative story. How the heck do you live under the authority of a story? Of a poem or a parable? How is a violent story about war or genocide authoritative? Do you just take the explicit commands and obey those? Which ones? Can we pick and choose?

The Bible's commands are right and fitting within their place in the story's context. The story documents commands for ancient theocratic Israel that don't apply to the characters in the New Testament, let alone to the Bible's readers centuries later on the other side of the world. But this only becomes a problem when you treat the Bible like a manual for life in the modern world rather than a story.

In a story, what's important for a character on page one is usually very different from what's best for that same character in act three. That doesn't mean that the things in the first chapter are bad or mistaken—they had their place in the story, and they communicated true things in their context—or that the story doesn't have any commands for modern readers. You just have to learn how to read it.

Reading the Bible is complicated, and it freaks people the heck out. Leviticus? Mildew? What? Rules about mildew? And menstruation? Is this real? And you have Bible scholars saying, "Look, that's not for us in the directly applicable sense." And then critics come along with the charge, "You're cherry-picking the Scriptures!"

But it has nothing to do with reading Leviticus and saying, Ew, no thank you. It's about understanding the grand, sweeping story and understanding our place in it. So, certain cultural symbols have evolved over time. When Paul and Peter "command" the church of the first century to greet one another with "a holy kiss," they are tapping into an important and appropriate gesture for their time and place, not instituting a specific and everlasting command for the church.

The same is true with things like head coverings for women or the dynamics between slaves and masters. It's actually a pretty short list. But just because we aren't meant to obey these commands with exact cultural specificity doesn't mean they are altogether meaningless. We translate them into our own time and place. It may no longer make a lot of cultural sense to go around kissing everyone, but we can greet those in the church with warm affection, kindness, and familial love.

And look, even if you make your peace with the Bible on the Bible's terms, you won't have it easy. There are poems about sex, poems about murder, God making bets with Satan, a guy living inside a sea creature for three days, and other miracles including but not limited to water turning into wine, sticks turning into snakes, rivers turning into blood, and dead people turning into people who are not dead at all.

Eventually, we have to admit that the Bible must have some level of irresolvable mystery. Why else would we have hundreds of splintering denominations and movements and theological perspectives and systems? That's a fair question, but honestly, it can be a tad overstated. When it comes to core theological essentials, pretty much everyone agrees that the Bible is very clear, and for two thousand years, there has been a historic Jesus tradition, and orthodoxy, that still holds to the way that the Bible has always been read.

And we understand that even when the Bible is as straightforward as it can be, we tend to cloud our interpretation of it with all kinds of baggage and bias.

But in my experience, the weird peripheral stuff in the Bible can be a challenge, sure, but most of the big-time crises I see around biblical authority aren't about interpreting obscure rules and holy war. More people have problems with some of the Bible's naked prose because they just don't like what it has to say. They tell me: "I just didn't *feel* like this was right."

A desperation for something else to be true. Something more accommodating. And they look, squinting as if into one of those Magic Eye images until they see something else entirely. Like a blacksmith with the Bible on an anvil, they hammer it into the shape of an echo chamber: It says what you're saying right back to you. It says what you want it to say.

It's a very American way of approaching the Bible. Thomas Jefferson famously cut out every part of the Bible he didn't like until he felt nice and affirmed about what was left.[6] Jefferson's bossy, entitled approach to this ancient library is alive and well in the deconstructionist movement, an indelicate, boorish clobbering to which progressive spirituality issues a bizarre and contradictory permission slip.

Remember, the Bible was not written by White people, nor by people with power, privilege, or social standing. Author Brian Zahnd summarizes the Bible's perspective this way:

> One of the most remarkable things about the Bible is that in it we find the narrative told from the perspective of the poor, the oppressed, the enslaved, the conquered, the occupied, the defeated. . . . We know that history is written by the winners. This is true—except in the case of the Bible it's the opposite! This is the subversive genius of the Hebrew prophets. They wrote from a bottom-up perspective.[7]

Most deconstructionists I talk to don't take this into account while they deconstruct. They're mad at the parents and pastors who slapped them around with the Bible, and they take it out on the poor and oppressed people who wrote the Bible. The deconstruction fad is about as American as baseball and apple pie.

Elsewhere in the world, the historic way of Jesus continues to thrive amongst people who don't happen to be hip, moneyed Americans with podcasts and verified blue checks on Twitter. They clamor, teary-eyed and shaking, over their first personal copies of the Scriptures. They huddle together under cover of night to avoid persecution just to be able to open this sacred, dangerous book. And here comes the young, enlightened American, wagging a disapproving finger at a book written by the poor and the oppressed, by people of another culture and color, this young American telling them how stupid they are, how misled.

Professor A. J. Swoboda points out that

> if I—a white Christian male—were to take elements of someone else's culture and use them for my own purposes, they would call it "cultural appropriation." But if I take the ancient writings of the Bible and change them to fit my purposes with no regard for the intent with which they

were written, they call me "enlightened" and "evolved." How could this be? [8]

He concludes:

> For every millennial, affluent, white college student who is choosing to deconstruct their Christian faith, there are five nonwhite people with less privilege in this world who are finding in the Bible the greatest message one could ever imagine.[9]

Even with a rich library of mystery and questions, beautiful and ugly, simple and profound, we can learn to open these pages and say, I don't get all of it, Jesus, but I'm learning to trust you.

It was Jesus, after all, who brought me here in the first place.

Complex feats of artistic genius have always fallen victim to misinterpretation, and people often blame the work itself rather than the person misinterpreting it. That doesn't mean that you have to fall before the Bible, miserable and prostrate, hating every second of it with no choice but to bow to its horrible authority. It means that entering into the process of interpretation takes time, community, and a willingness to meet the story on the story's terms.

The Bible's ideal reader refuses to become soft-minded and unthinking, just as they refuse to become cynical and suspicious. It's hard for us to release the death grip on our felt need for control, fast answers, and confirmation bias, and reading the Bible requires that we part with all three.

THE SECOND GREAT PREDATOR: THE PROBLEM OF EVIL

"It is not God who kills the children. Not fate that butchers them or destiny that feeds them to the dogs. It's us. Only us."

—ALAN MOORE, *WATCHMEN*

Chapter 5

CATS, COSMIC HORROR, AND CHAOS MONSTERS

I'M ABOUT TO MENTION a few horrible things. You can skip ahead to page 94 if you want, but at the end of these horrible things, I want to say something important about God.

The thumbnail was of a cat taped to a broomstick, and I couldn't sleep that night. This, of all things, became an evil too heavy for my faith to carry.

Animal rights groups were making phone calls to Toronto, to Montreal, looking for the YouTuber responsible for a series of kitten snuff films. This guy, whoever he was, was feeding kittens to a python, filming the whole thing, and uploading the clips to the internet. A few months later, the infamous and at large internet cat killer graduated from animals to humans (as is typically the case with people who hurt animals) and he uploaded a video of that too. The police caught him in Berlin, where he stopped at an internet café to google himself.

I was following the story in the winter of 2010, and I couldn't get that thumbnail out of my head. The cat, wide-eyed and panicked, taped to a broomstick before it was drowned in a bathtub, haunted my imagination my days. It was weird, me being bent out of shape like this. I'd seen worse.

I don't know why some of us have what is often termed a "morbid curiosity," but I do think that the whole thing is completely misunderstood. A morbid curiosity doesn't describe demented fetishists and gorehounds who thrill at the idea of blood and violence and tragedy. I won't pretend to know what makes such a person tick.

But most people, when they learn about something horrific, they say, "Spare me the details." Most people, if someone begins to detail suffering, death, and real-life horror, they say, "That's enough." I've been accused of having a morbid curiosity because when I hear about something awful, I lean in. When someone summarizes a tragedy, I go searching for the details. I ask questions like, How'd they do it? With what? What people don't understand is that I don't do this because I *enjoy* these hideous dark pockets of the world. I do it because I hate them.

When I hear about the worst things, I think to myself, What was that like? What if that had been me? What if that happened to someone I love? I go exploring the black hole like a dentist probing a cavity with a hook, wanting to know how bad it can get. Like Clay in Bret Easton Ellis's novel *Less Than Zero*, "I want to see if things like this can actually happen. . . . I want to see the worst."[1]

Plumbing the depths of the world's evil is one way I attempt to penetrate the world's pain. Anymore, it's getting hard to care, what with the livestreamed suicides, televised beheadings, and near-daily mass shootings. I'm being bombarded on all sides by doom every day. When a story comes to me about murder or abuse or a child with bone cancer, it seems wrong to keep such a powerfully painful thing sequestered in the unfastened safety of a headline, in some far-off story, sparing myself the bloody details, and proceeding with my otherwise comfortable day.

So, I keep reading until it hurts. Until I feel all of it. Not because I want to, but because I don't. I'm not constantly chasing after this stuff; it just finds me from time to time.

I don't know why the cat taped to the broomstick crippled my faith in the winter of 2010. I've seen and read about things that, according to the measuring stick by which we calculate evil, are much worse. It was the smallness of the act, I think, that bothered me. The horrible YouTube video that made headlines was an unpleasant reminder of the kind of world in which we live. That this kind of thing is happening in the dark corners of the planet, and most of the time, there's no video, no manhunt, no justice. Somewhere, someone tapes a terrified cat to a broomstick and drowns the animal in a bathtub, and the world goes on spinning in cruel indifference. The panic in the cat's eyes, for me, was a kind of cosmic horror, a sort of existential dread.

I was Ralph in *Lord of the Flies*, staggered by the darkness nestled in the hearts of men.

Literary enthusiasts will tell you that it's not the monsters that make H. P. Lovecraft's stories so scary. It's what the monsters imply. The monsters themselves don't really headline a Lovecraft story. Instead, the stories are about being driven to madness by the realization of something terrible: monsters exist. Like a wife who finds an earring that doesn't belong to her in her husband's sock drawer and is seized with an immediate, all-encompassing dread. It's not the earring that has, in a moment, shattered her world. The earring is a keyhole through which she is made to eye a world she never knew existed, a new world that brings the old one to an awful end.

When we talk about evil, we usually rush to Nazis and A-bombs. Someone asks, if God is all-powerful and all-good, why is there evil in the world? Right away, someone brings up Auschwitz. Right away, someone mentions 9/11 and civil war in Syria and dictators and nuclear explosions because of the undeniable scope of their wickedness. But this seismic evil carried out by soldiers and governments often detaches from the senses of ordinary people who can't imagine real-life mushroom clouds, crumbling skyscrapers, and emaciated children shuffled into gas chambers.

It was the panicked look in the cat's eyes that really bothered me, how helpless it was, unable to comprehend what was about to happen. I wondered what God had been thinking at the time, watching it happen, and like the awful earring of unfaithfulness uncovered in the husband's sock drawer, a horrible black ink seeped into everything.

My memory hovered over every sickening story in the archives of my mind, all the unimaginable horror that unfolds not on the blood-soaked beaches of Normandy, but in the unassuming quiet of suburbs and apartments, in backyards and basements and living rooms. I thought of the kind of cruel horror that erupts not in war zones or death camps but in what should be the domestic safety of a mother's care. I thought of the mom who, in 2004, severed her baby's arms from the infant's defenseless body, believing God had told her this was an important thing to do. I thought of the mom who woke her little boys in the middle of the night, lead them into her front yard, and smashed their heads with a landscaping stone. The children were found lying dead in their underwear, their skulls caved in near garden signs that read, "Mom's Love Grows Here" and "Thank God for Mothers." Another mom in Texas, I remembered, made headlines after dismembering and cannibalizing her newborn at the devil's behest.

I wondered how God felt, having to watch all that.

I thought of the famous musician who groomed his fans who were mothers to sexually abuse their small children. I thought of the Australian man imprisoned in the Philippines for operating a dark web child pornography ring, selling videos of his own creation that showcased the rape and torture of girls as young as a one-year-old baby.

I remembered reading that one of his victims told police, "I hope I can forget when I grow up."

I wondered how God felt, hearing that little girl say that.

The week I was writing this, a man strolled into a supermarket where he shot and killed a woman, her one-year-old grandson, then himself. The act, it seems, was completely random.

I thought of all this ridiculous random evil as a purposeless chaos monster, twisting up into the fabric of life itself like a parasitic vine and filling the bones of children with cancer, steering a drunk driver's car into a single mother of three on an evening stroll, in the wrong place at the wrong time. Somewhere, chaos rolls a rock down a cliff-side to crush a passing family in their truck. I thought of evil so absurd and so arbitrary that one struggles to blame anyone but God, like a cresting wave that swallowed up a man and his daughter near my home in the Pacific Northwest so that a teacher was made to explain to students on a Monday morning why their classmate's tiny desk would remain empty.

I thought of evil as a cruel lottery, remembering two young women who were camping in Morocco when strange men invaded their tent, raped and decapitated them while shouting, "Death to the enemies of Allah!" I wondered if maybe they'd camped a mile in another direction, or on another night, they'd have made it home with pictures to show their friends.

I wanted to be serious about the Bible. I didn't want to become dazed by the oldest question in the book and swallowed up by the chaos monster, but I was starting to feel dizzy, and somewhere in the shadows ahead, something was licking its chops.

The Apprentice: A Snake on the Road

THE YOUNG APPRENTICE WAS met on the road by a gliding Snake. The Apprentice was afraid, so he asked the Master, "Will you protect me from the Snake?"

The Master said that he would.

The Snake reared up, flashing curved egg-white fangs that dripped blinking stalactites of venom. Its scales glittering in the moonlight, the Snake seemed to rise and grow until it obstructed the path before the Apprentice.

"Master," the Apprentice said, his confidence shaken, "will you protect me from the Snake?"

The Master said that he would and continued on.

The Apprentice slowed to a stop, calling to the Master, "But I am afraid that if we continue on, the Snake will strike me."

The Master turned to face the Apprentice and said, "It will."

The Apprentice was afraid. "If I head back, I can escape the Snake's bite."

The Master shook his head. "The Snake will be there also."

"I think that I might flee."

The Master extended a hand to the Apprentice. "Come, follow me."

On the Master's hand, the Apprentice noticed two puckering craters of scar tissue, a snakebite.

"Master," said the Apprentice, "why do you let the Snake wander free?"

The Master stepped closer to the Apprentice, a sad smile on his face. "The Snake didn't always bite. It wasn't always a Snake. It was made good, free to go this way or that way. Like you."

The Apprentice was angry. "The freedom you granted the Snake has put me in danger! You say that you will protect me, but you also say that the Snake will bite me. I'm confused and afraid."

The Master's expression was gentle, full of compassion. "Love is dangerous. The Snake will bite you, and the bite will be painful, but I have nullified its venom so that the power of death is no longer in it."

Again, the Master extended his scarred hand to the Apprentice.

Chapter 6

GOD OF EVIL

In the winter of 2013, I learned to hate hospitals. I was a new father, my son only weeks old, when death moved in on heavy black wings over the Christmas season.

My dad was about to die.

He'd come to meet his new grandson, flying thousands of miles from Savannah, Georgia, to Portland, Oregon—a trip neither he nor my mom had braved until then, neither really being the traveling type. Setting foot on the West Coast for the first time in his life, my dad looked like the Georgian he was, stubbornly sporting shorts and flip-flops in near-freezing weather. Though Portland's yuppie hipsters were eager to compliment his long, graying beard, dad might've been wearing the only NASCAR hat in the city.

Already a profound lover of all things Christmas, I had a particularly full heart that December, remembering the strange and wonderful story of an all-powerful God who chose to become a helpless human infant, as nightly, I cradled a helpless human infant of my own. I loved my newborn son in a way I couldn't help but experience as a reflection of the good and loving God who felt so near at Christmastime. Then Dad got sick.

THE MANIAC GOD

English comedian and outspoken atheist Stephen Fry was once asked what he might say if, upon dying, he was confronted by a God who was very real after all. Without hesitating, Fry answered:

> I'd say, bone cancer in children? What's that about? How dare you. How dare you create a world in which there is such misery that is not our fault. It's not right. It's utterly, utterly evil. Why should I respect a capricious, mean-minded, stupid God who creates a world which is so full of injustice and pain? [1]

The journalist squirming in his chair, Fry explained himself. "Because the God who created this universe—if it *was* created by God—is quite clearly a maniac."

Mr. Fry was entirely correct. His outrage was justified. But that's not really a great reason to be an atheist or to abandon Christianity—as has been the case for so many deconstructionists troubled by the problem of evil.

Answering the problem starts with an ancient text from the Hebrew Scriptures, in the tenth chapter of a book called Daniel. As the story goes, Daniel gets bad news from God about an impending war. He responds appropriately with certain spiritual disciplines of abstinence and prayer. A bit later, we learn how God responds.

> Do not be afraid, Daniel. Since the first day that you set your mind to gain understanding and to humble yourself before your God, your words were heard, and I have come in response to them. But the prince of the Persian kingdom resisted me twenty-one days. Then Michael, one of the chief princes, came to help me, because I was detained there with the king of Persia. (10:12–13)

In ancient Hebrew thinking, the "king of Persia" isn't an actual human ruler on a throne but a spiritual being with authority over a geographic location. A territorial spirit. In this story, Daniel prays. He asks God to do something. Anyone who's ever prayed for anything can wrap their head around that one. Three weeks pass with no discernible response from God at all, and my guess is that anyone who's ever prayed for anything can wrap their head around that one as well. But as the story goes on, we learn that God had responded immediately—he dispatched a spiritual being (an angel) as an answer to Daniel's prayer. And yet, the response in question was delayed—not according to God's mysterious purposes, but because an opposing being in the spiritual realm delayed it.

God answered right away, but spiritual conflict interfered.

If something we can't even see (one spiritual entity resisting another spiritual entity) can delay an answered prayer, could the same thing stifle a prayer altogether?

Has this happened to you? How can you know? And if a spiritual being can do that, what else can they do? What else *have* they done?

For many, this is an unthinkable way of understanding the world. For others, the paradigm itself isn't necessarily a new one, but actually *living* as though this paradigm were true is a different story. Everyone is troubled by the bad things that happen in the world, but the Bible's explanation for this mess that we're in isn't what many people think.

DYING AT CHRISTMASTIME: DECEMBER

Mine is a personality haunted by death. I think, talk, muse, and joke about death more than the average person, I guess. I wouldn't say that I'm obsessed, but I am fascinated by this dark inevitability awaiting us all—that we can neither see nor know it until we're standing at the gates.

Even for someone who thinks about it quite a bit, death is an unwelcome guest, especially at Christmas. On December 24, 2013, I was staring at two empty seats while I tried to get my mom on the phone. The church where I worked hosted a big Christmas Eve party in downtown Portland, something I looked forward to all year. My wife was next to me, cradling our tiny son. "Where are they?" she's asking me. "Maybe they got lost?"

I'm thinking, *No big deal.* I'm thinking, *They probably got lost.*

My mom wasn't answering because she was driving my dad to a nearby emergency room in a strange city unknown to both of them. Dad had mentioned mild cold symptoms the day before, and when the sun set one last time before Christmas, he began to experience hallucinations.

As I'm singing hymns of worship to the benevolent God of the universe who came to bear our burdens and carry our pain, a doctor is telling my mom, "Things don't look good."

As I'm singing, "Repeat the sounding joy," the doctor is telling my mom, "The chances of survival at this point are 40 percent."

DEVIL

The primary antagonist of the Bible's story is a creature called the devil. In the Bible's worldview, the universe is made up of two overlapping realities: the physical realm and the spiritual realm. Both domains are populated with very real living beings with the power to interact with and affect both dimensions of reality, for better or for worse.

This means that we, as human beings, can interact with and affect the spiritual realm—pray against demonic oppression, ask for God's help, that sort of thing—but this is a two-way street. Just as we can interact with and affect the spiritual realm, the spiritual realm can interact with and affect us.

Spiritual entities can affect matter.

In the Bible, the things we can't see can interact with the things we can see. And in the same way that there are human and spiritual beings on God's side, there are human and spiritual beings set against God.

Apprentices of Jesus call them "the enemy."

The Bible describes this enemy as chiefly concerned with the work of stealing, killing, and destroying things (see John 10:10). His go-to strategy is deceit, but that isn't the only thing he does, and it certainly isn't the only thing he *can* do (see John 8:44). There are three complex categories at work in the world's ills: (1) sickness and death, (2) natural evil, and (3) chaos.

Building out these three paradigms is the work of constructing something called a *spiritual warfare theodicy*.

A *theodicy* is an answer to the problem of evil. The problem of evil is this: If God is all-good and all-powerful, why is there evil in the world? How you answer that question is your theodicy.

In Mark's Gospel, a man brings his ailing son before Jesus. The father claims that an evil spirit has made his son incapable of speaking, that it "throws him to the ground," in fits of convulsing hysteria. Mark claims that "the spirit" can see Jesus through the boy's eyes and that the boy begins to seize at the mere sight of Jesus. In response, Jesus "rebuked the impure spirit. 'You deaf and mute spirit,' he said, 'I command you, come out of him and never enter him again.' The spirit shrieked, convulsed him violently and came out" (see Mark 9:14–29).

Was the boy in the story sick, or was he being terrorized by an evil spirit? The father in the story describes his son as being "possessed by a spirit that has robbed him of speech." The malady is twofold: physical ailment/demonic oppression. In our postenlightenment modern world, we tend to dismiss the "evil spirit" prognosis as a primitive one. We figure the boy was probably epileptic and mute. Ancient peoples associated these kinds of things with "evil spirits" all the time, but *we* know better.

But in the story, Jesus doesn't chalk it up to seizures and antiquated medicine. He responds to the ailment by performing an exorcism.

And in the story, it works.

The boy (who had been mute) shrieks. Mark—the first-century biographer documenting the incident—doesn't depict Jesus as simply healing epilepsy. There are lots of stories about that kind of thing, but this isn't one of them. Instead, Jesus speaks directly to a personified entity, saying: "I command you, come out of him and never enter him again." So, was Jesus healing a mute boy, or casting out a demon?

According to the story, both.

It may seem bizarre, what I'm doing in this chapter. In a book designed to address misgivings so many people harbor toward the historic Christian tradition, I'm going on about an invisible spirit giving a kid a seizure. And though I don't really think that the spiritual realm worldview is as tough a pill to swallow as some make it out to be, that's not really the point.

MAD AT A COW FOR NOT BEING A DOLPHIN

A friend of mine works with an organization that hosts conversations about faith and spirituality. The format is simple: A curriculum introduces ideas about Christianity for group discussion, and a group of non-Christians discusses them. There's no correcting allowed, no arguing, no theological debates. The Christian host can't dominate the conversation. The material sort of speaks for itself and the participants are treated like grown-ups with agency, leaving the dialogue to go wherever it goes. Following this unconventional formula, tons of people decide to follow Jesus by the time the curriculum comes to an end. It's the least heavy-handed evangelism I've ever heard of.

A few weeks into his first venture leading the program, I asked my friend how things were going. Turned out, most of the men and women who'd signed up were no strangers to Jesus and the Bible. Most of them were jaded former Christians who had deconstructed their faith and registered for the course ready to come pick a fight. Every one of them had fallen before the same Great Predator.

The Problem of Evil.

No honest person can argue that the problem of evil isn't a real problem. The world is overflowing with unspeakable horror. Even those of us having a pretty even go of this thing called life have to admit that somewhere nearby, someone else is suffering.

Thing is, the small troop of angry former Christians gathered around a table with my friend were all mad about something many (if not most) Christians *don't actually believe*. As they launched their calculated attack against my friend—the Christian hosting the class—they were baffled to learn he agreed with them. All of them had been disenchanted by a paradigm they were handed somewhere along the way: a god who exercises total unilateral control of an evil world. But that all-controlling god is strangely absent from the Bible. They were, in essence, hurt and frustrated with a cow for not being a dolphin.

You can deem the Bible's story problematic and unbelievable—lots of people do—but I've met scores of people over the years who are mad at the Bible for things the Bible doesn't say.

There are, of course, Christians who believe God specifically plans, ordains, and controls everything from the flight patterns of dust particles to the gas chambers at Auschwitz, but for hundreds of years, no Christian believed such a thing. In fact, by the time Augustine proposed an all-controlling god at the center of the broken universe, his problematic deity was unanimously rejected by an official church council.[2] Christians who still insist on an all-controlling god (usually operating under the label of *reformed* or *Calvinist*) would probably admit that their theological tradition isn't exactly famous for its humble approach to doctrine, which explains why so many former Christians who bailed out on the all-controlling god had no idea there was any other way to understand him.

They abandoned Christianity hating an unknowable god who predestines mass shootings and damns children to hell before they're ever born. I don't blame them. I hate that god too. The Bible is very aware of all the horrible things constantly unraveling in our broken world, but it never blames them on the good God whom Jesus called "Dad."

This is why the Gospel authors want us to see Jesus's work of healing sickness and casting out demons as irrevocably connected ideas. Jesus didn't wander around ancient Palestine trying to undo God's work. For Jesus, disease and suffering and death are not ordained by God. They aren't God's will or plan at all, but the work of someone the New Testament calls the devil. He's given the title "ha-satan," which means "the adversary."

The Satan.

Of course, this worldview is not unique to one Gospel story. The authors of Scripture, the first disciples of Jesus, and the earliest church fathers believed the same thing articulated in Acts: "God anointed Jesus of Nazareth with the Holy Spirit and power, and how he went around doing good and healing all who were under the power of the devil, because God was with him" (Acts 10:38).

For the authors of Scripture, Jesus's work in healing the sick is not dissimilar to his work casting out demons. In Luke's Gospel, Jesus prefaces the healing of a stooped woman by asking a rhetorical question: "Should not this woman, a daughter of Abraham, whom Satan has kept bound for eighteen long years, be set free on the Sabbath day from what bound her?" (Luke 13:16).

The first important point in building a spiritual warfare theodicy is this: spiritual beings can afflict human beings with physical and mental illnesses. This point presupposes the belief that just as human beings have been created with agency—meaning, freedom to do what they want—spiritual beings have been given the same autonomy. Why? Couldn't God just get what he wants by exercising unilateral control over creation?

Well, sure, but then there would be no *relationship*, no *collaboration*, no *love*, and God's great desire for dynamic relationship is on fantastic display from Genesis to Revelation. We can approach the cosmic mystery of our broken world with a pretty simple rubric: everything God wants and does is always good. Because God is loving and personal, he made human beings and spiritual beings with genuine freedom to align themselves with what God wants and does *or not*. When these free beings exercise their freedom in such a way as to *not* align themselves with what God wants and does, the things that happen are *not good*. The world suffers. God wants peace, but we often want war. God wants life, but human beings often want death. God wants little boys to be healthy and capable of speech, but spiritual beings (who come to steal, kill, and destroy) want them to be sick and mute. God has no mysterious purpose behind evil because he's not responsible for any of it. Look at the way C. S. Lewis summarizes the idea:

> God created things which had free will. That means creatures which can go either wrong or right. . . . Free will, though it makes evil possible, is also the only thing that makes possible any love or goodness or joy worth having. A world of automata—of creatures that worked like machines—would hardly be worth creating. The happiness which God designs for His higher creatures is the happiness of being freely, voluntarily united to Him and to each other in an ecstasy of love and delight compared with which the most rapturous love between a man and a woman on this earth is mere milk and water. And for that they must be free.
>
> Of course, God knew what would happen if they used their freedom the wrong way: apparently He thought it worth the risk. . . . If God thinks this state of war in the universe a price worth paying for free will—that is, for making a live world in which creatures can do real good or harm and something of real importance can happen, instead of a toy world which only moves when He pulls the strings—then we may take it it is worth paying.[3]

DYING AT CHRISTMASTIME: JANUARY

Every patient in the intensive care unit that Christmas had been toppled by influenza. They were all dying from the flu. I had never heard of such a thing. I'd never been inside an ICU, and I remember surveying the landscape of unconscious bodies and asking a doctor in disbelief, "The *flu*?"

"It's a bad one this year," was all she could offer in reply.

They shaved my dad's beard so they could push a ventilator down his throat. The first time he regained consciousness inside the hospital, he stared at me, trapped behind a fog of sickness and drugs, not recognizing his own son.

It was another bad sign, they told me.

Dad had likely caught the flu on his flight across the country. Because he had failed to care for his body over the years, this particularly nasty strain of influenza was teaming up with diabetes and heart disease to drag him into the murky shadow of death. I was making nightly trips to the hospital after work as the short holiday visit my parents had planned became a miserable stretch of anxious weeks without end.

I think I prayed with more passion and conviction in those weeks than ever before. I immersed myself in worship and meditation, not to curry God's favor, as if he would only answer a good little boy who read his Bible every morning, but because I was desperate and scared. I was not particularly horrified by the idea of death, and I knew that my parents, like all of us, would die someday. But to go out like this? To catch the *flu* on what should have been a short holiday visit to hold a new baby and to die afraid and confused in a strange city with a plastic tube forced down your throat—it all seemed particularly cruel, and I didn't want it to happen.

I remember taking deep breaths as I parked at the hospital night after night, reciting psalms aloud, pleading with God for a miracle, for healing. I remember sending updates to friends and family I knew were similarly crying out to God for something to change. I remember constantly answering the same stupid questions posed by well-meaning acquaintances, exhausted by everything. Day after day, my chest tight and my legs shaking, I went back to the hospital—past the front desk, left down the hallway, not the first set of elevator doors but the second one, several stories up, through the sliding glass doors and into the mocking threat of encroaching darkness.

I had to admit that during these miserable weeks, I somehow felt closer to God than I'd remembered feeling in a long time. Just as my small, fragile son depended on his father's strong arms to carry and care for him, I was helpless against circumstances beyond my control, and I nestled myself into the arms of God and went on praying, helpless and afraid.

One evening as I stood bent in a hospital doorway, a doctor told me my dad had been awake earlier that day, lucid but confused, surrounded by masked strangers and the low hum of soulless machines. "He asked for you," the doctor told me. "When he was awake, he was asking for you."

CHAOS

From the Bible's opening story to its triumphant conclusion, it argues that both human and spiritual beings have freedom, both capable of good and evil. So, as far as the Bible is concerned, the spiritual and physical realms are two distinct but overlapping realities. We interact with the spiritual realm, and it interacts with us. The Bible presupposes much broader implications of this arrangement than most people assume. It's not just people caught in the cosmic cross fire of freedom run amok. The entire natural order suffers the consequences of evil. In Romans, Paul talks about the creation itself waiting in eager expectation for a day when the broken way of things is no more. He describes creation as being subjected to frustration by an outside force, hoping to be "liberated from its bondage to decay" and made free. The whole creation, Paul writes, "has been groaning" in anticipation. Every cell, plant, animal, every blade of grass desperate for the end of death and decay (see Rom. 8:18–22).

There are creatures in the animal kingdom—parasites—that feed off other living things in grotesque and ultimately fatal ways. The ichneumon wasp is an insect that lays eggs in the body of a living host so that its hatchlings devour the host alive from the inside before erupting from its body like something from a David Cronenberg film. While studying the ichneumon wasp, Charles Darwin struggled with his dwindling belief in a good God. He wrote to a friend:

> I am bewildered. I had no intention to write atheistically. But I own that I cannot see, as plainly as others do, as I wish to do, evidence of design and beneficence on all sides of us. There seems to me too much misery in the world. I cannot persuade myself that a beneficent and omnipotent God would have designedly created the Ichneumonidæ with the express intention of their feeding within the living bodies of caterpillars, or that a cat should play with mice.[4]

And to another friend:

> What a book a Devil's chaplain might write on the clumsy, wasteful, blundering low and horridly cruel works of nature![5]

Many creatures abandon, kill, even devour their own newborns. The natural world is often a violent and cruel nightmarescape overflowing with abject suffering. And the animals are only one aspect of what we call *nature*. There are hurricanes, tornadoes, volcanoes, tsunamis, earthquakes. Why?

The early church uniformly argued that spiritual beings (like humans) were created free and that they, like humans, are granted influence and responsibility in the created order. In John's Gospel, Jesus describes the devil as "a murderer from the beginning" (8:44). Meaning, the devil was already bringing forth death and destruction before we got here—a murderer from the *very* beginning.

To understand the problem of evil as the Bible understands it, we need something called a spiritual warfare theodicy. In a spiritual warfare theodicy, spiritual beings can afflict the natural order—creation itself—with evil, suffering, and even death.

These are the first two building blocks—that the autonomy of human beings and spiritual beings creates the possibility for sickness and death, and that spiritual entities can affect the natural world with evil and suffering. Then, the final piece: chaos.

A popular figurehead of the deconversion movement is Dave Bazan. He practically wrote the soundtrack for the deconstruction movement. Once lauded for lending credibility to the mostly dismissed idea of Christians making indie music with artistic integrity, Bazan chronicled a very public, very ugly breakup with God on his 2009 album *Curse Your Branches*. In the song "When We Fell," Bazan vocalizes the same old objections to the all-controlling god of his church upbringing, understandably concluding that if God determines all things, certainly he is to blame for the terrible human predicament.

If God's determinative will is the ultimate source of genocide, racism, and children being raped, it's not exactly shocking to behold legions of would-be Christians heading for the exit. Being discouraged by a hard-to-believe setup in which an invisible devil is up to no good is one thing, but being mad at God about the devil's work is another. Many of us have only been offered one extreme or another. Either God controls everything—including the devil—or the devil is the convenient scapegoat for everything from a cough to a parking ticket.

The quest to find balance in the supernatural worldview often declines inside a frustrating nebula. If you set out to join Jesus and the early church in taking the supernatural realm very seriously, you probably also want to avoid becoming the type of person who blames the devil for anything and everything that isn't entirely awesome, as if you are being personally antagonized by Satan when you spill your coffee.

And that brings us to chaos.

A branch of mathematics called chaos theory argues that any complicated system can be massively affected by seemingly insignificant happenings along the way. The slightest variation in a sufficiently complex process at one point may cause remarkable variations in that process at another. This is sometimes called "the butterfly effect." The flap of a butterfly's wings in one part of the globe can, under the right conditions, be the decisive variable that brings about a hurricane in another part of the world several months later.

Here's why this matters.

In the Bible's story, our world, our lives, our own souls are broken. Bent out of shape. Bent away from what is true and good and toward that which destroys us. We've done one hell of a job, so to speak, tearing the world apart. Because both humans and spiritual beings are created with freedom, and because that freedom is often used to do evil, creation itself pays an ongoing price. We're all caught in the cross fire. In the world we know, YouTubers drown cats, children are abused, wasps lay eggs in caterpillar larvae, hurricanes destroy civilizations. The world is ravaged by evil and suffering and death.

All of us know from experience that even a seemingly insignificant act of evil—a cutting word, a fractured relationship, a lie—doesn't exist in a vacuum. It has consequences. The same is true on a cosmic scale, from relational exchanges to eons of natural evolution. Simple actions set in motion ripples in the water of the universe, and those ripples intersect with others. In our world infected by evil, we are often victimized by that evil simply because of complicated and indifferent patterns of chaos.

It's not God's plan, but it's not always the devil's plan in the specific sense either. Sometimes it's just a clustercuss.

So, when I use the word "demonic," I might mean it as direct and indirect. Direct demonic oppression is obvious enough. It's the exorcism stories of Jesus. It's probably a lot of the horrifying and unimaginable things that send the world reeling in grief and outrage, like mass shootings and child abuse.

Indirect demonic oppression is any and all kinds of evil that—for all we know—may not be personally energized and enabled by an evil spirit, but it is demonic simply because evil itself is, by biblical definition, demonic.

Evil originates in Satan and his kingdom.

In both cases—direct and indirect demonic activity—disciples of Jesus follow in Jesus's example by recognizing evil for what it is and where it comes from. Theologian Greg Boyd says it like this:

> When one possesses a vital awareness that in between God and humanity there exists a vast society of spiritual beings who are quite like humans in possessing intelligence and free will, there is simply no difficulty in reconciling the reality of evil with the goodness of the supreme God. . . . It virtually sidesteps the problem of evil.[6]

DYING AT CHRISTMASTIME: FEBRUARY

Two months after my parents arrived for their holiday visit, our prayers were answered. My dad was pronounced healthy enough to leave the ICU and begin physical therapy at a nearby recovery ward.

His beard was gone, his voice hoarse, his frame enfeebled from inactivity, but dad was back. We celebrated Christmas in February, all of us packed into his little room, his electric bed crowded with gifts.

I was overcome with gratitude deep down in the depths of my soul that morning. The collective prayers and petitions of so many faithful Christians had not fallen on deaf ears—God had intervened! A man with dismal chances of survival was laughing with his family, celebrating a Christmas the doctors believed he would likely never see. Christmas! The great reminder of God's closeness—God *with* us—and he was.

After a stint in recovery that seemed fleeting compared to the ICU's soul-draining crawl, my dad was cleared to travel home. We were laughing about everything by then, the insanity of it all, and I hugged my dad goodbye as spring began to thaw the bitter cold of winter.

It was the last time I would ever see him alive.

WHAT GOD CAN'T DO

I know a young woman who embarked on a very vocal deconstruction of the Christianity in which she was raised. As she dissembled her parents' faith brick by brick, she found new holes in the infrastructure every step of the way. Eager to celebrate her newfound spiritual freedom to anyone within earshot, she would detail the hard proof of God's inexistence with anecdotes about unanswered prayer.

"Every night," she said, "*every* night, I would pray with my daughter that she wouldn't have any nightmares. But she kept having them!"

Case closed. No God. She'd been lied to.

This brittle paradigm of prayer betrays a significant misconception about the way God has arranged the universe. It's easy to see why. Part and parcel of Christian doctrine is the relevance and power of prayer. In Christian theology, God is not distant nor aloof but intimately involved in even the minutia of our everyday lives. Christians believe in prayer, but we also have no choice but to acknowledge the reality of prayer that remains unanswered. This young mom asked God to stop her daughter's nightmares, but her daughter's nightmares didn't stop. Is it that God didn't care about a child suffering nighttime distress? Did God determine those nightmares with some mysterious intent beyond our understanding? Or was it something else entirely?

If part of our broken creation is inherently chaotic in the wake of autonomous wills, infinite variables, demonic influence, circumstance, and natural evil, how does God intervene? When we pray for protection, or against evil forces, or for healing, or for other people to come to faith in Jesus, how does God respond?

In his book *Letters from a Skeptic*, Boyd likens prayer to wartime communication. Imagine, he says, a home surviving a season of war in occupied territory. This home is made up of the wife and children of a head captain who is currently away at war against the invading enemy.

Imagine that in this family's home is a small radio that communicates with a device that the captain carries on his person while he is away at war. Let's say the family radios the captain to inform him that they've fallen victim to an attack, that they need supplies, that they're wounded. The captain hears the request and cares tremendously for his family. Even so, he is a part of a larger battle, with thousands of lives to consider, presumably some immediate skirmish the moment he was radioed.

Sometimes the captain meets his family's requests, and sometimes immediately so. Sometimes he answers, but his answer is delayed (as was the case with Daniel's angel). The family lacks the captain's broad perspective, so they trust that the captain cares for them, wants to meet their needs, and works to do so with every resource at his disposal. But it isn't possible for the captain to intervene in every way, even the way he'd like to.

I know what you're thinking about Boyd's metaphor. You're thinking, "God is different than this captain," right? For one, God is all-powerful. So how can something be "impossible" for God, as it were? Think about it this way: Though we all know what we mean, collectively, when we say something like, "With God, all things are possible," it's not really true in the exact sense. These kinds of deep truth statements are not intended as precise metaphysics. Consider, for example, that Christians believe that God cannot sin. God cannot be tempted, James says. God cannot violate the law of contradiction. He can't make a round triangle.

There are things God can't do.

Similarly, God cannot sovereignly decree a cosmos that is both free *and* not free. If the cosmos is free, then by definition, human beings and spiritual beings are free to do something or not do something. If God intervenes in such a way that he decrees we can *only* do this thing and *not* that thing, then we are no longer free. God can do anything he wants, so he could have arranged the universe differently, but this loving, personal God desired relationship. And like C. S. Lewis said earlier, "For that, they've got to be free."[7]

For God to respond to every prayer in keeping with his heart, he would have to revoke freedom, nullify relationship, and violate the law of contradiction. As far as we can tell from the Scriptures and our own experience, he doesn't do that. Irrevocability is built into the definition of free will. This means that you and I are confronted with life in a world that is wonderfully free but consequently chaotic, riddled with evil, and set before the inevitability of all kinds of suffering, and ultimately death. (At this point, I'd like to note that I am also available to officiate weddings.)

Still, in my mind, the inevitability of suffering is not a realization without hope.

Christians love to go on about victory, which puzzles more than a few non-Christians when the world doesn't seem to reflect any Christian victory to speak of. One way of understanding the entire biblical narrative is that it is the story of an ongoing cosmic war.

The war has been won, but the fighting hasn't stopped.

We've seen this idea play out before in the theater of war. On June 6, 1944, the allied forces stormed a beach in Normandy, France, and overcame the German military there. Historians tend to agree that this day on the beach was the decisive victory moment of World War II, and yet it took another year for the war to come to an end.

Once more from Boyd:

> Christ in principle defeated the powers with the unsurpassable love he unleashed through his incarnation, life, ministry, death and resurrection. D-day has been fought and won. But we are still waiting for V-day. In the meantime, there are many important battles to fight. Indeed, sometimes an enemy fights the hardest when they know their doom is certain.[8]

In our story, the hero has already rescued his love, but the battle rages on. The enemy has been defeated, and on a coming day, *all* of the enemy's evil will be completely eradicated for good, and the war will come to a conclusive end. For now, sometimes life feels as if it is bathed in the future hope of total victory, and other times it feels trampled beneath the unforgiving parade of defeat. We're still waiting, but we have hope.

The Great Predator of the Problem of Evil devours so many would-be disciples of Jesus because it confuses the Creator God with the one Paul calls "the god of this age" (see 2 Cor. 4:4). Anyone would be well within their rights to feel angry about the awful state of evil in the world, but if you're going to get frustrated with God or the Bible, at least understand where both localize the onus of responsibility for this mess. One of the most essential aspects of overcoming this Great Predator is understanding what the devil does, and what God does, and how the two are never alike.

In the words of Jesus himself: "The thief comes only to steal and kill and destroy; I have come that they may have life, and have it to the full" (John 10:10). One brings death, the other life. Fundamentally opposite poles.

God's purpose for you is not death.

My heart breaks and my stomach turns when some vile thing happens in the brokenness of our world—a mass shooting, a hurricane, a child beaten—and I hear the old adage that has become the inroad for innumerable deconstructions: God is sovereign. God is in control.

No. God doesn't do those things.

I once sat and listened as a man stood before a congregation and claimed that though his father had physically abused him for years, God had orchestrated each beating with a great purpose in mind.

No. God did not do that. A broken man did that, and he carried out the will of Satan, not God.

The distinction matters.

How can anyone go to battle with an enemy if they attribute his work to God's will? To God's control or mysterious purposes? How can anyone hope to understand God if they impose on him the murderous work of the Evil One?

At the time of writing, my kids are still pretty small. Once, when I was wrestling with them, my daughter inadvertently injured herself. A minor injury, but she cried. And in her tears, she said, "Dada *pushed* me!" I held my sniffling daughter in my arms and said, "Dada did not push you. Things were crazy, and you fell, but it wasn't Dada." A silly sounding analogy, I know, but as a dad, I felt a horrible pang at my daughter's briefly held assumption that I had intentionally hurt her.

Can you imagine how God the Father must feel to have the devil's work attributed to him?

Following the Japanese tsunami of 2011 in which nearly twenty thousand men, women, and children were killed, there were, of course, pastors and thinkers who spoke up to attribute the tsunami and its effects to the work of God. Theologian David Bentley Hart became so deeply troubled by this claim that he authored a small book in response. In this scathing indictment of the all-controlling god, Hart writes:

> If indeed there were a God whose true nature—whose justice and sovereignty—were revealed in the death of a child or the dereliction of a soul or a predestined hell, then it

would be no great transgression to think of him as a kind of malevolent or contemptible demiurge, and to hate him, and to deny him worship, and to seek a better God than he.[9]

About eighteen pages ago, I argued that Stephen Fry was correct in his denouncement of the evil god behind bone cancer in children. The Bible tells a story about an evil being at work in the universe, the god of this age. This evil god's work is indeed revealed in the death of a child, the dereliction of a soul, and the horrors of hell. And indeed, it is no great transgression to think of him as a kind of malevolent lesser god, and to hate him, and to deny him worship, and to seek a better God than he.

Mr. Fry was entirely correct. He was just talking to the wrong god.

To the god responsible, I join Mr. Fry in saying: Bone cancer in children? How dare you. But this is not my God. This evil lesser god I denounce just as I denounce his work and its toll on our world.

DYING AT CHRISTMASTIME: MARCH

Often, I have heard the expression, "No parent should ever have to bury their children." The implication being that children are meant to bury their parents and not the other way around.

This is wrong.

Parents should not have to bury their children. Children should not have to bury their parents.

In the midst of personal tragedy, the suffering and traumatized begin to hear vague spiritual platitudes on the lips of well-meaning comforters. "God is in control," they say. "God has a plan." And though the sentiment nestled within such expressions is sometimes charitable and good, a sinister inference swallows any kindness in its ominous shadow, as if God himself might tower over our misery as a terrible grim reaper, distributing calamity and injustice at his own dreadful whimsy.

This is, of course, untrue. Reasoning of this kind terrorizes Scripture, devastates the character and goodness of God, and levels any cheap, short-term comfort it affords with its abominable consequences.

Death is not God's plan. It is not his will, not his intent, not his best. For followers of Jesus, death is an enemy. An enemy whose parade of affliction, misfortune, and sorrow defies the God of love. Death happens against God's will, in rebellion and defiance of God's will.

But not for long. No, not for long.

Because the hope for followers of Jesus is not that evil and calamity are somehow grafted into God's good plan for humanity, but that no matter what evil befalls us, God is at work to bring good out of that which violates his will. What a far more glorious comfort to extol a good and gracious God at work in a fallen world—a God who subverts horror and creates goodness—lest we warp his character into a monstrosity that orchestrates evil and death in order to meet his ends. As if these ends might only be met if God were pulling all the strings.

No, God did not kill my dad.

When my phone rang late one night in March of 2014, I knew something was wrong. My stomach sank when I saw my sister's name on the caller ID. When I didn't answer, she called again.

Earlier that night my dad had hobbled to his bed to rest, and when my mom went to stir him, she found him dead. "He was already cold," was how my sister put it, crying into the phone that night.

The floodwaters of grief had burst forth from the precarious enclosure of a life without tragedy. Rather than toppling the humble house of my faith, my theology of suffering became a powerful bulkhead, diverting the awful surging sea, and though it passed over and through me, the house of my faith did not fall.

Days later, I was in Georgia again. For the first time in many years, I warmed the sanctuary pews that once tested my capacity for belief. Before I was to speak, the same pastor who declared me apostate as a teenager rose to the pulpit to pray.

"God," he declared, "is sovereign over death. The Lord gives, and the Lord takes away."

Moments later, I preached to a church that likely doubted I would ever do such a thing anywhere, let alone there. "No," I said, my voice reverberating off the century-old wooden walls. "No, God did not take my dad."

No, Satan is likely not responsible for every bad day and headache, but all that is not good is either directly or indirectly connected to the Evil One, and I will blame God for none of it. And when we are berated with stories of marriages undone by unfaithfulness, and relationships broken by selfishness and deceit, of mass shootings and injustice and police brutality, of children abused or neglected or starving, of foster children waiting in an office terrified and suddenly homeless—I recognize God is not the one "in control" of these things. They belong to the Evil One.

But not for long.

I join with my teacher, my Master, my Lord Jesus in rebuking him, pushing his parade of darkness and despair back as I await a coming day when Jesus will crush the Serpent's head once and for all, and the Serpent will never steal or kill or destroy every again. The Father of Lies comes to do these things, but Jesus comes to give life and life to the fullest.

I stand with him, and the once Great Predator falls before me.

Part Two

DECONSTRUCTING HUMANITY

"I think there is no suffering greater than what is caused by the doubts of those who want to believe. I know what torment this is, but I can only see it, in myself anyway, as the process by which faith is deepened. A faith that just accepts is a child's faith and all right for children, but eventually you have to grow religiously as every other way, though some never do. What people don't realize is how much religion costs. They think faith is a big electric blanket, when of course it is the cross. It is much harder to believe than not to believe."

—FLANNERY O'CONNOR, *THE HABIT OF BEING*

(Before We Continue)

As a writer, I found the suicide notes exhausting. There was all this pressure to say the most important things I would ever say, and all this shame from admitting to myself that no matter how eloquent the suicide letter, anyone reading the thing would come away thinking, "He didn't love anyone or anything enough to stay."

Hunter S. Thompson gave his suicide note a title, even though the whole thing would fit on a Post-It. "No More Games," he wrote. "No More Bombs. No More Walking. No More Fun. No More Swimming." He called the note "Football Season Is Over," which, I think, is an excellent title for something despite the fact that I don't really know anything about football or its seasons.

I was trying to keep them short, direct, write them all by hand. Then I'd think of something to add, and I'd need to start the whole thing over. Maybe, I thought, I should type them first and *then* reach for a pen.

It started with all the lists I was making, trying to think of anyone I felt was owed a unique explanation as to why I'd given up on everything. I knew the letters wouldn't help, but I figured saying something was better than leaving without a word.

So, I figured I'd write one general letter, you know, to everyone, and then a handful of other letters I would leave for close friends and family. I was asking myself ridiculous questions, like, Will so-and-so be offended if such-and-such gets a suicide letter, but they don't? I scrawled notes in the document I'd made to keep up with everything.

The document had headings like "pros," "cons," "further research," "to-do," and "possible dates."

Under "possible dates," I wrote, "June 12, 2018." My birthday. Birthdays of deceased loved ones, I knew, could be difficult, but so was the anniversary of their death. It made practical sense to combine the two and save everyone a day of obligatory grief. This is good, I thought. Getting organized.

Like all disciples of Jesus, I'd gone through faith and doubt and cynicism and despair, but without denouncing Jesus. I'd prided myself on my willingness to endure without bailing, but I had been looking into the abyss for so long, indulging in it, that it had begun to warp my perception of just about everything. I wouldn't have admitted it then, but in my own way, I was preparing to denounce Jesus once and for all. I was preparing to execute the ultimate and most final deconstruction.

I couldn't see it because I was still reading my Bible, still praying.

I was talking to God through all of this. Talking but not listening. I was still smiling and nodding and laughing with friends. I was often happy beneath the black canopy of my despair. No one knew I was making a list. Every day when I'd come home from work, I would see my little son staring out of the living room window, waiting on me to arrive. Every day he'd run to the car, calling for me. His face beaming, he'd climb into the front seat before I could even unbuckle.

I was talking to God through all of this. Talking but not listening.

In seminary, I took a class on suicidal ideation and prevention. One therapist I read about would threaten to starve the cats of her suicidal patients.[1] To that despairing, suicidal patient, she'd ask, "Yeah, but if you kill yourself, who will feed your cat?"

And when the patient thought about it, they might say, "I'll ask my mom to feed my cat."

But the therapist was always one step ahead of them. "I'm going to call your mom and tell her not to feed your cat."

This is very similar to how God lifted me from the black mire I'd been wallowing in. This is how God took me by my shoulders and shook me and leaned in close with a face so stern and so severe that, for a moment, the heavy gloom lifted from my eyes and God gave me an image so stark and so vivid that in a moment I felt a clarifying jolt. The road of discipleship—a road I was preparing to abandon forever—opened before me once again in all its narrow, winding, uneven glory, and I found tired strength in my legs, hobbled to my feet, and staggered forward on a familiar path that, time and time again, seemed somehow new.

THE THIRD GREAT PREDATOR: A POLITICIZED CHRISTIANITY

"Let him begin by treating the Patriotism . . . as a part of his religion. Then let him, under the influence of partisan spirit, come to regard it as the most important part. . . . Provided that meetings, pamphlets, policies, movements, causes, and crusades, matter more to him than prayers and sacraments and charity, he is ours–and the more 'religious' (on those terms) the more securely ours. I could show you a pretty cageful down here."

—C. S. LEWIS, *THE SCREWTAPE LETTERS*

Chapter 7

COCAINE MELTDOWN SOMEWHERE IN MIDDLE AMERICA

I WOKE UP IN a van somewhere in the Midwest. It was late, but it was hot, and I was sticky with sweat. What woke me up was that the guy in the van next to ours was having some kind of meltdown.

I was blinking hard, trying to wake up. The van was parked in a row of other white fifteen-passenger vans that looked exactly like it along the load-in zone of another crappy theater. A band was playing inside, all thundering bass and growling vocals. Teenagers and twenty-somethings littered the lot, smoking cigarettes, drinking beer from clear plastic cups. Everyone looked like they really dressed up for this, the show, with very cool outfits, hair teased and dyed. Everyone was looking at me, so I thought I better put on a shirt. I was tired, and I wanted to take a nap before our set, but now I figured I was going to have to sign CD covers, and I wasn't really in the mood.

Only no one was looking at me or caring about my signature. They were looking at the guy in the van next to ours having his mental breakdown. He was usually high on something—this guy in this other band on tour with us—and he was prone to fits, but this one seemed particularly nasty. His girlfriend was pacing around the locked van, screaming at him.

"Stop it, Jonathan! Just stop it, okay?"

But he went on shrieking and slamming his head against the windows until there was blood on the glass.

Someone should do something about this, I thought.

Jonathan, high on something, had become convinced that his girlfriend was cheating on him. Maybe she was and maybe she wasn't, I don't know, but he didn't exactly seem an authority on reality at the moment, squawking like a seabird and smashing his forehead into shatterproof glass.

"I wasn't *doing* anything!" his girlfriend was screaming.

Jonathan flipped onto his back and started driving both feet into a van window like a jackrabbit.

"Are you kidding me, Jonathan?" his girlfriend said, hands on her head like a distressed cartoon character.

I was looking for my shirt.

I heard some kid in the parking lot say, "This is more entertaining than their set!"

Kids can be so cruel.

The door opened beside me, and Ivory told me we went on in fifteen minutes. He was my oldest friend, Ivory, and we'd been traveling like this for years now. Ivory asked, "What's with Jonathan?"

"I think he's high or something," I said.

We both winced as the window Jonathan had been kicking erupted in a spray of shattered glass. Ivory looked out over the people scattering throughout the parking lot and said, "Those are supposed to be shatterproof," then he looked back at me and said, "Fifteen minutes."

I went back to searching for my shirt.

We'd been at this for a while now, the whole traveling circus thing. Mostly, you live in a van, driving from city to city, state to state, day in, day out for weeks, months at a time. Sometimes we flew on airplanes to other countries, and as we wheeled our cheap suitcases into an airport terminal, we were vibrating with anticipation. Then we'd touch down in another country, rent a van, and resume the same cycle of driving, sleeping on floors, eating bad food, wanting a shower and not getting it.

For many years, I liked this very much. Things started to unhinge, and I liked that too. But behind the veil of sideshow lunacy, other things were collapsing. Everyone was leaving home as a Christian, but fewer and fewer people were coming back that way.

Patrick started buying economy-sized boxes of matches at gas stations. He'd light them and throw them at whoever was trying to sleep. The only way to beat him at his own game was to light yourself on fire. So, on long, boring drives, Mike would hold a cheap orange lighter to the corner of his T-shirt, and the whole thing would go up in flames while he was still wearing it. All of us roaring with laughter, Mike would scream and flail, panicked, trying to thrash his way out of the burning shirt, tearing at it like someone in one of those animal attack videos. All of this is happening in the back of our van, coasting through the line at a 24-hour drive-through while whoever is driving yells, "Hey! Everyone shut up! Yeah, can I get two cheeseburgers, please?"

Other things happened.

We traveled with a Daisy Red Rider BB gun and played games of UNO where the first person out got to shoot the last person in. We shot ourselves and one another in an attempt to discover what area of the body (below the face) was most vulnerable to BBs. (It was the thumbnail at point-blank range, and yes, we tried everything.) We ruined things on purpose. A big group of us would cram into a mall photo booth, pooling together our last few dollars for a picture no one needed. The moment the photo fell from the machine, we grabbed it and tore it to pieces, all of us snickering like gremlins. This was our idea of funny. Funny kept things in motion. If everything is a joke, why be mad? Why freak out? Why bother with homesickness or travel fatigue or exhaustion or malnutrition or crises of faith or cokeheads who shatter van windows when everything is a joke?

You can't live like this forever. People were changing. No one was emotionally healthy or mature. I think we loved each other, but we didn't know how to navigate or resolve conflict, so we were cowardly, passive-aggressive, cruel. Incapable of sincerity, nothing mattered. Anyone who showed their belly was ridiculed for it. I wondered what we believed sometimes.

Somewhere in the Midwest, Ivory told me he was leaving. We were standing next to someone's pool, the teal surface crowned with dead leaves and algae. "I think it's time for me to step down," he said. He was unknowable to me in that moment, that he could imagine a world beyond this one.

The whole thing, the fire-breathing misadventures of a few young men, had started with us praying. The narrow confines of our insular Christian world had chewed us up and spit us out, propelling us into the big bad world. Somehow, my faith was fortified. But now it had been years since the era of rubbing alcohol and a crumbling mobile home. I had found in punk rock an electrified connective tissue to express what I believed to be the truly subversive teaching of Jesus. Now, even in our tiny indie corner of the music industry, things were starting to feel safe. The routine became predictable. Drive, eat garbage, play at some sweaty dive, sleep on some painfully uncomfortable floor, repeat. For a while, we held nightly Bible studies. At first, this was rejuvenating, then a staleness settled over everything until it became an empty, begrudging obligation, mostly rushed.

But we did it, and didn't that count for something, God?

Our peers were dropping like flies. When we set off, there were so many of us, like-minded in our enthusiasm for Jesus and punk rock—the artistic and evangelistic marriage of the two. Now thousands of miles from their families and pastors and youth groups, the Jesus thing seemed less interesting to just about everyone we knew. What was more interesting was alcohol, sex, cocaine hysteria, and a kind of lived nihilism. The other bands, the ones who left home Christian but didn't return that way, they'd see me carrying my Bible into dressing rooms and hotels, and they'd ask, "You still believe in that stuff?"

Before all this, we'd survived our hometowns and backwoods churches, and we'd seen the problems, the sanctimonious, superficial Christian culture, the Bible wielded like a weapon for proving points and winning fights. But now, we were seeing that weaponization organized on a massive international scale. What was once our small, tattered canopy of Christian culture revealed itself as an imposing umbrella stretching out from sea to shining sea, and the umbrella was red, white, and blue.

In America, the escalating drama of the 2000 presidential election became a reckless cyclone moving through the balsa wood façade of evangelicalism, dismantling any pretense of fidelity to Jesus, any veneer of authentic Christianity. God was at war against Democrats, left-wing values, and progressivism, and he was out for blood.

We were seeing behind a curtain, and what we found made us want out.

For the first time in our young adult lives, we would find ourselves of voting age in a culture war. God, we were learning, was more concerned with American politics than just about anything in the known universe. Things were getting ugly, and the wind of that ugliness was staggering fragile Christians, fresh out of the nest, walking a precarious tightrope. If they'd been teetering before the fall of 2001, a storm was coming to clear the tightrope altogether.

The Apprentice: Crowding Battalions

THERE CAME ON THE road of apprenticeship a sound like thunder. On the horizon, a marching infantry, their boots like hammering pistons in the dirt. The soldiers came beneath flags decorated with the image of a tiger. Raised high on gleaming iron poles, the flags rippled in the air above them as they came.

The Apprentice turned to his Master, but before he could speak, the battalion had crowded around him, obscuring the Master from sight.

"Who do you fight for?" one of the soldiers shouted at the Apprentice.

"I am walking with my Master," the Apprentice answered.

"You do not *walk* with the Master. You *fight* for him!"

Roars of approval rose up from the other soldiers. The Apprentice could see that their flashing swords were speckled with blood. The tiger soldier said, "Our battle is against the jaguar soldiers."

"But my Master said that we are to love our enemies, that we fight with weapons of peace . . ."

"Weakness!" the tiger soldier interrupted. "You would have those who hate the Master make a fool of him and us!" The soldier leaned in close, sneering at the Apprentice. The soldier said, "The Master's enemies will have his teaching wiped out, if we do not rise up to vanquish them!"

The Apprentice searched the road for his Master, but the fuming flag-wavers continued to eclipse the Master from sight.

The tiger soldiers pressed their case. "Do you care nothing about the jaguar soldiers who would normalize sin, rewrite the nuclear family, take our guns, and remove prayer from schools and football games?"

Then a new voice called out from a distance, "Liars!"

A brigade of new soldiers beneath a jaguar flag marched into the fray, shouting at the tiger soldiers. "These dogs are no moral guardians! They care nothing for the poor and the oppressed, only for violently imposing their religious dogma on others!"

"Godless heathens," sneered a tiger soldier.

"Backward bigots," growled a jaguar. "These evil hate-mongers must be silenced and banished from society! Their White, cis, heteronormative patriarchy is on the wrong side of history!"

The Apprentice thought of how the Master promised to unite his people despite preciously held beliefs that once kept them at each other's throats. These soldiers claiming the Master were anything but united.

Beyond the throng of radicalized patriots, the Apprentice could see a few would-be apprentices idling down the narrow road, looking for the Master. When these curious would-be apprentices saw the loud, ugly mass of soldiers crowding the road before them, they stopped walking. The Apprentice worried he would be mistaken for a soldier.

For a moment, he considered turning back.

Without moving forward, without trying to make sense of the mess before them, the discouraged would-be apprentices turned and went back the way they came, repulsed by the anger and violence that seemed to block the way forward. The Apprentice called out to them, telling them that neither he nor the Master belonged to these tiger or jaguar flags. No one seemed to listen.

The Apprentice listened for the Master, but it was hard to hear much of anything except the soldiers shouting over one another, so the Apprentice grit his teeth and pushed forward.

"You'll never follow the Master unless you follow us!" shouted the tiger and jaguar soldiers as the Apprentice escaped the tangled mass, leaving them to their shouting match, an ugly obstruction on the road.

Then he could see the Master again.

Chapter 8

BAPTIZED IN EMPIRE

READ ABOUT THE FIRST century and you can travel backward in time to a place called Thessalonica, this little city nestled within the larger kingdom of Macedonia, home of Alexander the Great. But Macedonia was eventually invaded, overthrown, and occupied by the Roman Empire. It was the dawn of a Roman era. Thessalonica was chosen as the capital city of the newly Roman Macedonian province.

Little Thessalonica felt pretty special, being a new capital and all. For all its special treatment, there developed in Thessalonica a decidedly pro-Roman disposition. We like the boss. Eventually, Rome declared the new capital a "free city," and Thessalonica became tax-exempt and independently governed. She could mint her own money, and she was free from Roman occupation. The only catch was this: You can have it nice, but only so long as you maintain allegiance to the Roman Empire. Rome won't micromanage your way of life just so long as you remember who is in charge.

And Thessalonica remembered well. Archaeologists have uncovered evidence of an imperial cult in Thessalonica—people who actually worshipped the emperor as a god. Caesar Augustus's image replaced the image of Zeus on Thessalonian coins. Statues of Augustus depicted as divine were stationed throughout the city. The looming presence of the emperor was inescapable.

This was the gospel—the good news—of Caesar's reign.

Thessalonica was officially free, at a cost. City officials were expected to encourage and enforce loyalty to the emperor to maintain the peace and keep the city within his majesty's good graces. Their way of life was contingent on allegiance to god and country. *God* being Caesar, *country* being Rome.

The city's leaders instituted oaths like this one:

> I swear . . . that I will support Caesar Augustus, his children and descendants throughout my life in word, deed, and thought, . . . that in whatsoever concerns them I will spare neither body nor soul nor life nor children, . . . that whenever I see or hear of anything being said, planned, or done against them I will report it, . . . and whomsoever they regard as enemies I will attack and pursue with arms and the sword by land and by sea.[1]

Today, immigrants to the United States are made to pledge a similar oath:

> I hereby declare, on oath, that I absolutely and entirely renounce and abjure all allegiance and fidelity to any foreign prince, potentate, state, or sovereignty; . . . that I will support and defend the Constitution and laws of the United States of America against all enemies, foreign and domestic; . . . that I will bear arms on behalf of the United States when required by the law.[2]

Or, in children's classrooms across the country, an oath to an idol: "I pledge allegiance to the flag . . ."

Read about the first century, and you can travel backward in time to a place called Thessalonica: pagan (not Christian), pluralistic (a culture of many gods), hedonistic (if it feels good, do it), and steeped in nationalistic idolatry (religious allegiance to politicians, parties, policies, and country).

(Or, if you're an American reader, no need for time travel. Just stay where you are. You already get the idea.)

Into this first-century world of paganism, debauchery, and Caesar worship stepped a Jewish rabbi turned missionary for Jesus called Paul, with a dangerously subversive message. You can read about it in Acts. The news about Jesus creates such a divisive uproar in Thessalonica that the Christians are brought before city officials. The charge is made: "These men who have caused trouble all over the world have now come here. . . . They are all defying Caesar's decrees, saying that there is another king, one called Jesus." At this, the gathering crowds and authorities are "thrown into turmoil" (see Acts 17:6–8).

Here, in the beginnings of the Christian movement, already there's criminal sedition. We think of uprisings and rebellions, and we think protests, riots, Molotov cocktails. But often, the most subversive and effective rebellion is the simple defiant act of telling a different story. Paul and his friends arrived in Thessalonica without hashtags or gas masks or flags on their pickup trucks, but armed instead with a different story. We have good news about a new king, and his name isn't Caesar.

People lost their minds. They still do.

Caesar demands allegiance and a way of life, but Jesus makes a competing demand for the same things. Only one master can be obliged. So, naturally, in the story, Paul and his friends attract attention, get into trouble, and are banned from Thessalonica as enemies of the state.

Read about the first century, and you can travel backward in time to find a peasant stonemason turned Jewish rabbi called Jesus of Nazareth, who was executed by the Roman Empire for criminal sedition. He was an enemy of the state. You'll see that Jesus's earliest followers were similarly understood as liabilities—dangers to the political machine. Possible insurrectionists. You'll see that as the Jesus movement proliferated across the ancient Mediterranean, the early Christians were eventually persecuted, arrested, and executed by soldiers, officers, and politicians.

And probably, you'll think, This is weird.

Really weird, given the fact that you'll also see that both Jesus and his earliest followers uniformly taught and practiced the ways of peace, nonviolence, and enemy love. Really weird, as Israel's Messiah, Jesus, was assumed to take up the mantle of a military warrior and arrange a violent political revolt against the oppressor, but he did not.

Jesus's disciples were accused of inciting protests and riots, of planning to overthrow the government—and not only did they do neither, but they also taught and promoted ways of life that made either thing an impossibility. They believed in keeping your head down, loving your enemies, leading a quiet life, and as long as the rules didn't require you to disobey Jesus, following them.

And then, you'll think, Things are getting weirder. You'll see that the political charges against Jesus and his earliest disciples weren't entirely without cause. The way of Jesus became revolution, but it wasn't the kind of revolution anyone suspected—then or now.

Take Thessalonica, for example.

By the time we get to the New Testament letter we call Thessalonians, Paul—the man responsible for planting a church in Thessalonica and writing a letter to it—has been kicked out of the city on suspicion of political subversion. And Paul did lead an uprising in Thessalonica, but it was somehow quiet, peaceful, and more revolutionary than any riot or violent revolt.

REVOLUTION IN SOUTHEAST GEORGIA: 1998

I'd bought a pack of T-shirt markers at the local craft store across the street from the dry cleaners where I was working at the time. In my bedroom that evening, I smoothed a cheap white T-shirt over a brown paper bag, and I took from the package the red and blue markers. Red, white, and blue.

I started by drawing a 'familiar image, something I'd seen all my life on T-shirts and bumper stickers. Something I'd seen flying high on innumerable poles in the tri-county area. It was the official flag of my high school and of the entire state of Georgia. I began with a big blue X, punctuating the crossbeams with thirteen white stars before framing the whole thing in a red rectangle. Eventually, the Confederate battle flag stared back up at me from the T-shirt in shining wet ink.

Next, I wrapped the entire flag in a red circle with a diagonal line running through it. The same angry red "do not" sign that warned of no-smoking areas and trapped the panicked white specter of the Ghostbusters logo. The no symbol. Beneath the defaced flag, I wrote, *heritage of hatred*.[3] I sat back on my knees and smiled at the finished product. The next day was a school pep rally. Hundreds of students—most of them Black—would crowd into the gymnasium as the marching band performed "Dixie" to soundtrack the screaming frenzy of crazed football players with cabled necks and sweat-beaded foreheads. They would brandish the Confederate battle flag, a totem of inevitable victory against some other school down the street.

This, I thought, was the perfect T-shirt for such an occasion.

Though the history of flags once waved by the Confederacy during the civil war is muddled to say the least, at some point, the Battle Flag of the Army of Northern Virginia became the stark emblem recognized the world over as "the Confederate Flag." The big blue star-spangled X on a red rectangle is every bit as polarizing as a swastika. As a child, I was promised this ubiquitous token had no wicked underpinnings, that it merely preserved a proud heritage. But I didn't have to travel beyond the backwoods world of southeast Georgia to learn that, for many, the "stars and bars" were an emblem of violent nationalism, White supremacy, and the Southern longing to return to an idyllic era of slavery, plantations, and cotton fields.

For most of the day, no one said anything about the vandalized Confederate icon on my T-shirt. Then, during lunch, a burly senior in a trucker hat caught a glimpse of the image and asked for a closer look.

"That," he said, pointing at the tarnished flag, "that is an ass-whooping right there." He walked away looking determined to arrange this very thing, and in moments my table was surrounded by a dozen very angry-looking young men.

"Take the shirt off," they were saying. "Take the shirt off *right now.*"

It's not that I was particularly brave. It was just hard to imagine a serious beating in the safety of the cafeteria, in plain view of the faculty and staff.

So, I just said, "No."

This parade of angry students followed me to my next class, skulking behind me as if to remind me of my encroaching doom. Word spread quickly. Classmates were either vowing to protect me or to destroy me. By fourth period, people were using the term "race war."

I thought, This is going better than I expected. I thought, I'll wear this shirt again tomorrow. It was, after all, spirit week.

By the time the local news station arrived at school to cover the incident, the principal was pretty upset with me. We went to the same church, my principal and me. I remember him saying, "That flag is your heritage," fury and hurt in his voice as if defacing the confederate flag was akin to spitting on the graves of his grandparents. "When you dishonor that flag, you dishonor American soldiers. You dishonor the state of Georgia."

I was squinting at his desk, confused.

"You're a Christian, son," he told me, like this was something I'd forgotten in my rebellious shirt-making zeal. "You're a Christian. You should act like it."

GARTH BROOKS AS POLITICAL INKBLOT TEST

When you lead a church, you have to make decisions. You lead Sunday gatherings and prayer meetings. You write sermons and sermon series. You plot a course for the vision of a coming week, month, year. You can't talk about everything. You can't even talk about *most* things. Sometimes things happen in the world, and you feel like, as a church leader, these things need addressing. People will disagree with your decisions.

In 2020, America (and really, much of the world) resumed an ongoing and controversial public discourse about race and injustice.

Many churches, including ours, participated in that conversation. And many churches I knew (including ours) were sometimes accused of becoming *political*. When people say this, they mean that you're losing your way. Going off the rails. There are areas of our lives we would rather Jesus's teachings not touch. All of us know this. It doesn't really bother us if Jesus issues a polite reminder to be kind, but he can mind his own business when it comes to sex. We like Jesus's teachings about love and peace, but we don't want him to tell us how to spend our money.

But he does.

Similarly, the way of Jesus is inherently political. But not in the way so many people seem to think. Theology is the study of God, and everything is theological. This is not hyperbole. The clothes you're wearing, the air around you, the grass outside, your schedule, your breakfast, aardvarks, Martin Short—*everything* is theological.

In my years of talking about the church and the state, I've gathered that what many mean by their accusation "this is getting too political" is that the person or church or artist being accused is articulating (or inferring) a political position at odds with the accuser's personal party or preference. It's not so much that the accuser takes issue with the idea of things "getting political," it's that, for them, things are getting political on the *wrong side*.

Get political in ways that happen to align with partisan allegiances, and you'll get a standing ovation. Get political in a way that doesn't outright celebrate precious party loyalties, and someone will bite your head right off.

I tend to think that when I've done a halfway decent job aligning myself with the teachings of Jesus, I will get angry emails from people on both ends of the political spectrum. It happens. Ask Garth Brooks.

In 2020, Garth Brooks—perhaps country music's all-time greatest— shared a photo on social media of himself in a football jersey intended to pay tribute to an athlete from the city in which he was performing. Said athlete's name is "Sanders." Barry Sanders. Barry Sanders's jersey number is 20. Thing is, Sanders is also the last name of a one *Bernie* Sanders, who also happened to be running for president in 2020.

Sanders, 20.

So, Garth's following lost their minds. Up and down the post, the overwhelming objection and outrage from Garth's fan base was, "Stop being political!" You just lost a fan, they said. Stick to music, they said. So disappointed, they said.

But Barry Sanders is a well-known and beloved athlete. The jersey and the name became an inkblot test. What do you see? A running back or a politician? An athlete or a socialist? People see what they want to see. On the other side of the aisle, a scattered few applauded Garth. Yes, they cried, seeing what they wanted to see. Vote for Bernie! For them, learning Garth Brooks had football on his mind rather than policy was a discouraging bummer. They came away frustrated that Garth was not the political hero they believed, if not for a moment, he might have been.

When you scratch at the idol, people freak out. The same thing happens to Christians and pastors and theologians and churches.

If you read Jesus long enough, he will have something to say about everything. You'll find all the obvious stuff associated with Jesus: love, forgiveness, mercy, etc. But then Jesus will have something to say about the way you organize your time and spend your money and express your sexuality. He'll want to talk to you about the things you eat and the way you treat the environment, about your lifestyle, and about your relationship with government and politics.

Few things press a person's theological squirm button quite like Christians talking politics. Who can blame them? For a few centuries, we've done a very, very bad job of it. The people who already believe that Jesus's teachings are inherently political tend to assume said teachings adhere to a party or a side or even a country or a particular system of government.

Sure, they say, Jesus is political. Of course he is! His politics are exactly like mine!

It's a bad look. Google any given survey of deconstructed Christians, and you'll find that among the top reasons cited for abandoning ship is a politicized faith. This is what twisted the thing we call evangelicalism into a political term—a hollow social expression of faux Christiandom not only dissimilar to the teaching of Jesus, the writings of the New Testament, and the practices of the early church, but antithetical to them.

The whole thing leaves a few of us hanging around, calling out to the long snaking line of disillusioned would-be Christians heading for the exit, pleading, "Hey! Don't leave on account of them!"

REVOLUTION IN SOUTHEAST GEORGIA: 2001

It was the phone that woke me. I crawled from a mattress on the floor to a ringing landline and, pressing the warm plastic to my ear, asked, "What is it?"

Mike told me, "We're under attack."

I asked him, "Who is?"

He said, "America."

That seemed pretty broad and pretty vague, but the barely functional tube TV in the living room of our trailer told us all about planes flying into New York skyscrapers, and for a long time, this horrible thing opened itself like spider legs over everything else happening in life and the world. People were talking about war and terror. Fear propaganda dominated every broadcast and public discourse. America was seething with a blood lust that could only be satisfied by bullets and bombs and the heads of people we didn't know, but we were told they were very, very bad.

The gas station down the street was selling cheaply printed T-shirts featuring the xeroxed-looking visage of Osama bin Laden with a bullet hole through his head.

No one knew exactly where all of this was going, really. Was another plane on the way? Something worse? Was my mail covered in anthrax? Were we headed to war? Was war headed to us? It was about to be a strange and chaotic season for America, marked by civil unrest and sociopolitical vitriol. The civil religion of American Christianity was about to take a hit, the shock waves of which would extend across the entire world for years to come.

Few things exposed the festering wound of politicized evangelicalism quite like an argument between civil rights leader Jesse Jackson and televangelist and political activist Jerry Falwell that aired on CNN in the fall of 2004.

Jackson argued, "Our going to Iraq was a misadventure. It has put America in isolation. We are losing lives, money, and losing our character in that war."

To which Falwell blurted, "I'd rather be killing them over there than fighting them over here."

"Let's stop the killing and choose peace," Jackson pleaded.

"Well, I'm for that too," Falwell began. "But you've got to kill the terrorists before the killing stops. And I'm for the president to chase them all over the world. If it takes ten years, blow them all away in the name of the Lord."

Maybe Falwell was agitated when he said it. Maybe if he'd calmed down, he wouldn't have said it. But it was too late. The words and everything they revealed had been vomited out and immortalized on live television. Jackson, visibly shocked by Falwell's audacity, could only reason, "That does not sound biblical to me. And that sounds ridiculous."[4]

Falwell's hellish, violent confession—to see all his perceived political enemies blown away "in the name of the Lord"—was the cancer diagnosis the country had been willfully ignoring until this satanic declaration rang out over broadcast airwaves round the world. It was like someone had burst into a dinner party and, in vivid detail, owned up to an affair everyone already suspected they were having. We knew something was wrong, but this was a bold and vulgar way to learn just how septic the infection had become.

All this was bad enough but imagine that at that same dinner party, with the blurted confession of infidelity still hanging in the air, one by one, other dinner guests speak up to confess their own affairs until most of the room is crowded with an ugly hopeless faithlessness.

My head was bleeding when I brought it all up.

We'd agreed to perform a 9/11 fundraiser of some kind. I'd thrown myself into our drummer and his drum kit, and my forehead had been on the receiving end of a cymbal's sharp edge. Everyone was a new kind of patriot in those days. There was a lot of "united we stand" talk. American flags stuck to everything. Throughout the show, every band offered some "go America" or "kill the terrorists" speech, the audience roaring their approval.

I don't remember exactly what I said. Everyone who knew our band knew that we were Christians, and Christians had been leading the angry "let's get 'em" mob with nooses and AK-47s. I wanted to say something.

I started some bit about forgiveness. About the way that hatred and violence tend to spawn on the damp basement floor of our wounded resentment. I said that only love and forgiveness could stop this angry, destructive cycle.

"Wait," someone said in the front row, plastic beer cup in hand. "Are you saying we shouldn't make the terrorists pay for what they did?"

Someone standing beside the guy came to my defense. "I don't think that's what he means."

"That *is* what I mean," I said. One or two people clapped. Slowly. A few people jeered. I didn't have a developed theology of enemy love back then. I hadn't even really formed the thought as it escaped my mouth and boomed out through the PA and over the little crowd. It just felt like something was wrong.

That thing—the wrong thing I could sense in the air—was an usher moving up and down the aisle of the rickety bus that was American evangelicalism, asking passengers, "Is this your stop?" To be a Christian in those days felt akin to demanding the head of Osama bin Laden on a platter through gritted teeth. The nebulous expectation of Christians as inherently political and inherently Republican was solidifying to the degree that all three were becoming interchangeable synonyms. Repulsed and discouraged, people were leaving the Christian bus in droves.

"Maybe one day I'll be able to claim Christianity *and* Christ," one friend told me. "But for now, I can only claim Christ."

Not long after that, he became an agnostic.

"I can't belong to a movement associated with George W. Bush," another friend confessed. "I love Jesus, but I am not a gun-toting right-winger."

She left the church, and in a couple of years, she'd become an atheist.

"For now," said a band I knew, "we're distancing ourselves from Christianity. We love God, but we can no longer confess this awful thing that Christianity has become."

All of them became atheists.

After that night in 2001, when I was rambling about forgiveness to a crowd drunk on beer and xenophobia, I was confronted by a fellow Christian. He touched my shoulder while I was hauling amplifiers into the back of our van. The blood on my forehead had dried to a burgundy crust.

"Everyone is upset," he told me, like this was something I'd forgotten during the spastic, sweat-drenched theatrics of the evening. "Even so, that kind of talk is disrespectful to our president and to our leaders and to victims of terrorism."

I reached for another amplifier, my headache returning.

"Everyone's upset," he said, "but you're a Christian. You should act like it."

GOD: THE RELUCTANT LIBRARIAN OF GOVERNMENT

I've gathered over the years that, for many, entertaining a calm and civil conversation about Jesus and politics is a difficult thing to do. There are all sorts of reasons. The way we've been raised. Our culture. The stories we've come to believe over time. The things we take for granted.

When it comes to parties and policies, people really want to believe Jesus is on their team and that he's really bent out of shape about the other team. The implication of a Jesus who isn't impassioned by the same political causes or disgusted by the same political opponents is, for many, crushing. Hint at such a thing and watch as hackles rise, defenses spike. Does Jesus watch CNN or Fox News? Does Jesus prefer millennial Instagram stories or boomer Facebook feeds?

Argue with someone about politics and the Bible, and eventually, someone will mention the thirteenth chapter of Romans. Romans 13 is often cited as *the* text on church and state, but more often than not, it's cited without mention of the chapter that precedes it, despite the fact that it belongs to the same unit of thought and teaching.

This is from Romans 12:

> Bless those who persecute you; bless and do not curse. Rejoice with those who rejoice; mourn with those who mourn. Live in harmony with one another. Do not be proud, but be willing to associate with people of low position. Do not be conceited.
>
> Do not repay anyone evil for evil. Be careful to do what is right in the eyes of everyone. If it is possible, as far as it depends on you, live at peace with everyone. Do not take revenge, my dear friends, but leave room for God's wrath, for it is written: "It is mine to avenge; I will repay," says the Lord. On the contrary:
>
> > "If your enemy is hungry, feed him;
> > if he is thirsty, give him something to drink.
> > In doing this, you will heap burning coals on his head."
>
> Do not be overcome by evil, but overcome evil with good.
> (vv. 14–21)

Because this library of writings is so big and complicated, our Bibles are all marked up with numbers and headers and footnotes. In the original text, there are no verse markers or chapter breaks, so Paul's train of thought flows immediately into what we now know as Romans chapter 13:

> Let everyone be subject to the governing authorities, for there is no authority except that which God has established. The authorities that exist have been established by God.
>
> Consequently, whoever rebels against the authority is rebelling against what God has instituted, and those who do so will bring judgment on themselves. For rulers hold no terror for those who do right, but for those who do wrong. Do you want to be free from fear of the one in authority? Then do what is right and you will be commended. For the one in authority is God's servant for your good. But if you do wrong, be afraid, for rulers do not bear the sword for no reason. They are God's servants, agents of wrath to bring punishment on the wrongdoer. Therefore, it is necessary to submit to the authorities, not only because of possible punishment but also as a matter of conscience.
>
> This is also why you pay taxes, for the authorities are God's servants, who give their full time to governing. Give to everyone what you owe them: If you owe taxes, pay taxes; if revenue, then revenue; if respect, then respect; if honor, then honor.
>
> Let no debt remain outstanding, except the continuing debt to love one another, for whoever loves others has fulfilled the law. (vv. 1–8)

Eventually, Paul offers the summation idea: "Love does no harm to a neighbor. Therefore love is the fulfillment of the law" (v. 10).

Romans 13 belongs to an unfortunate club of infamous Bible passages stripped of their context and twisted out of shape until they defy the teachings of Jesus and the other writings of the New Testament. It doesn't take any seminary gymnastics to explain the problem. Romans 13 is constantly wielded in such a way that it crumbles with even a surface inspection. A popular interpretation of Romans 13 is this: Paul intends to teach that government is ordained by God.

Thus, government activity—from policy to legislation to military violence—is ordained by God to accomplish the will of God.

Reading Romans this way, it logically follows that it is good for Christians to participate in politics, government, military, and so on. Many would go as far as to argue that to do so is the moral obligation of the Christian.

There's a long list of problems with this line of thinking. First, here's a fair question: Did Paul really mean to teach that all governments at all times are exactly as God intended them? That all governments exact the will of God? American Christians love to use this passage to enthrone their preferred president when that president is in power, but why stop there? Communist China under Mao? The Soviet Union under Stalin? Hitler's Third Reich?

Or maybe more acutely for Paul's writing, what about Emperor Nero? We think that a few short years after Paul drafted this letter, Nero became the first great persecutor of Christians—feeding them alive to wild animals and burning them alive as they were suspended on poles to light his garden at night. In this world of wild barbarism against Christians, disciples of Jesus would have been reading Paul's letter. These Christians who had witnessed members of their church and family burned alive or fed to lions, they would have read Romans 13, verse 1: "Let everyone be subject to the governing authorities, for there is no authority except that which God has established. The authorities that exist have been established by God."

What did *they* make of Paul's words?

The Greek word that my Bible translates as established is *tassō* (τάσσω).[5] It means "to draw up in order" or "to arrange." Some theologians have used the analogy of a librarian to clarify the meaning of *tassō*. A librarian arranges books. The librarian did not write the books. The library may well have problems with the books or find the books entirely contemptible—but the librarian knows that certain kinds of books go in certain places. So they arrange the books.

Though there are people who believe and teach that God is "in control" and that everything that happens—good or evil—is the outworking of God's "plan," for centuries of church history, no one believed that. For several hundred years of the early church, no one reading Paul's letter understood God's providence as unilateral control. They didn't clutch their crying children to their heaving chests as snarling lions inched forward, whispering, "God is in control. Everything happens for a reason."

This is the first glaring issue with the "God wants you to support government" interpretation of Romans 13. The early church did not believe that the evils of governments were the will of God. Just as God works in all of humanity's self-imposed chaos to maintain order without violating freedom and to bring good out of evil, he does the same within the broken institution of government.

The second complication is that, really, our metaphorical librarian didn't even want there to be books at all.

In the story of the Bible, ancient Israel, wanting badly to be like all the other nations, asks for a king. Up until then, there hadn't been a king, and Israel is sick of her own kinglessness. God is hurt by the request, going as far as to say, "They have rejected me as their king." God warns Israel, If you insist on human kings, they will "take your sons . . . to make weapons of war and equipment for [their] chariots." Israel says, Fine, whatever, we still want a king. They want government. They want human rulers to lead them into glorious military victory (see 1 Sam. 8). God, on the other hand, sees in the future of human government oppression and injustice.

God wants to be the king of his people.

That Israel gets a king at all is a concession. God is willing to work with and through broken people and systems, but from the beginning, humanity's desire for government has been an expression of their unfaithfulness to God.

Some things never change.

In the Bible, God does not propose human government. Humans do. And as is the case all throughout the Scriptures, God gets his hands dirty to work with his people in their brokenness. God could have told Israel, "Fine, whatever, have a king, but don't expect me to be around when it falls apart!" But instead, God graciously accommodates and collaborates, working within the madness and evil of crooked humanity, a master strategist wringing water from a garment soaked in sewage.

INVERTING THE POWER STRUCTURE

God doesn't ordain or control government. He works with government like a librarian, filing things, good or evil. And then there's the other major problem with the popular reading of Romans 13. The other major problem is the chapter before it.

In Romans 13:4, Paul claims: "Rulers do not bear the sword for no reason. They are God's servants, agents of wrath to bring punishment on the wrongdoer." If disciples of Jesus are somehow involved in this process, Paul is more than a little confusing. Just before this passage, Paul specifically commanded that wielding the sword as agents of wrath is exactly what disciples of Jesus are commanded *not* to do.

Remember?

> Do not repay anyone evil for evil. Be careful to do what is right in the eyes of everyone. If it is possible, as far as it depends on you, live at peace with everyone. Do not take revenge, my dear friends, but leave room for God's wrath, for it is written: "It is mine to avenge; I will repay," says the Lord. . . . Do not be overcome by evil, but overcome evil with good. (Rom. 12:17–19, 21)

In Paul's mind, God has always worked in and through broken systems as much as possible—without overturning human freedom—to maintain a semblance of order in a broken world. But the way God works through world government is very different—antithetical even—from the way God works through disciples of Jesus. Christians reject the sword (as Jesus commanded) and embrace peace and enemy love. The state doesn't do that. The state wields the sword. And yes, God is always at work to bring good out of evil, but disciples of Jesus "overcome evil with good."

Notice Paul's shift in emphasis. Watch the pronouns: "As far as it depends on *you* [Christians in Rome], live at peace with everyone. . . . If *your* enemy is hungry, feed them." Then in chapter 13: "Rulers do not bear the sword for no reason. *They* are . . . agents of wrath." Paul is saying, look, the world works this way, but you—Christians—you are to embody something else entirely. The state uses the sword, exacts revenge, represents wrath to maintain social order. They demand taxes and obedience.

The church, however, rejects the sword, leaves revenge to God, represents compassion, embodies self-sacrificial love, and willingly offers up taxes and submission.

Neither one can possibly do the other. It's not hard to see why.

All world governments influence behavior via the threat of punishment. Some are arguably more moral or less evil than others, but they all function this way. There are rules. "Law and order." If you break the rules, you will be punished by the sword (you'll be fined, imprisoned, or even executed). Every government on earth thinks they have the best vision of power. Every nation that goes to war thinks they're the ones on the right side. Then you read the New Testament, and you realize Jesus's vision for discipleship inverts the power structure.

Rather than the top-down power—coercing behavior, the threat of punishment—Jesus's kingdom functions via radical self-sacrificial love for others, including our enemies. These are things that the state—the empires and governments of the world—simply cannot do. World governments will never practice Jesus's teaching on nonviolence and enemy love, nor should we expect them to. The world's empires are not built on the foundational principle of radical self-sacrificial love that changes hearts but on power over others to coerce behavior.

The government does one thing. The church does something very, very different. For hundreds of years of church history, the earliest followers of Jesus deliberately and uniformly withdrew from the world of politics. Apprentices of Jesus were predominantly Jewish, belonging to a persecuted minority used and abused by the systems and institutions of power. They did not initiate violent revolt, and they did not stew in their hatred of the oppressor. In fact, from this small, persecuted rabble, we get writings like this one:

> I urge, then, first of all, that petitions, prayers, intercession and thanksgiving be made for all people—for kings and all those in authority, that we may live peaceful and quiet lives in all godliness and holiness. This is good, and pleases God our Savior, who wants all people to be saved and to come to a knowledge of the truth. (1 Tim. 2:1–4)

Writings like this one circulated in times of oppression and persecution that boggle the modern mind. The world of Jesus and his earliest apprentices was a sociopolitical nightmare overseen by bloodthirsty tyrants and pederasts who ruled with racism and injustice, oppressing the poor, the marginalized, and the foreigner. So why is there not a single recorded teaching from Jesus of Nazareth that encourages traditional political activism? Why did Jesus propose no adjustments to the system that so victimized his people? Why does the New Testament not mobilize the early church to legislate their way of life and take Israel back for God?

Why didn't Jesus rock the vote?

How foolishly unrealistic, how naive they seem to the modern reader. Pray for those in power? Bless and do not curse?

And yet . . .

The teachings of Jesus and the practices of the early church somehow changed the ancient world. These naive and foolish early Christians bypassed the political system of power over others and chose instead to serve and sacrifice and do justice.

And somehow, it worked.

The way of Jesus proliferated amongst dinner tables, from one home to another, bringing with it justice and reconciliation, uniting people of different ages, genders, nationalities, and ethnicities, turning the ancient world upside down. This unanimously understood distinction between the kingdom of God and the kingdom of the world lasted for centuries until AD 312 when Emperor Constantine claimed to receive a vision from "the Christian God" that he believed enabled him to emerge victorious from the Battle of Milvian Bridge. If Constantine did experience a vision that compelled him into slaughter, I doubt it was from the Spirit of God. Maybe something else. Something darker.

Either way, Constantine legalized Christianity via the Edict of Milan, and for the first time, the church got in bed with the empire. A veritable mountain of books and sermons have been devoted to dissecting the devastating effects of this moment in history—effects that linger to this day. But for hundreds of years, every disciple of Jesus believed that while the state did one thing, the church was to do something very different.

So, we have a problem.

REVOLUTION IN SOUTHEAST GEORGIA: 2011

Was it Prague or Vienna? I can't remember. Somewhere between France and Poland—a damp, miserable six-week trek across six or seven European countries—someone heckled us for being Christians.

This kind of thing happens all the time. It's no big deal. You'll be partway through your set, screaming your head off, drenched in sweat, when between songs, some jerk will scream unintelligible swear words from the peanut gallery, and you can tell from their voice that these particular swear words are derisive rather than celebratory. This guy, the one in Prague or Vienna or wherever it was, he was going on about bombs. I made a joke. We played the next song.

Afterward, I saw the heckler by the bar. I walked over and asked him what he'd been screaming, and he was, like most hecklers at punk shows, surprised, softened, and disarmed when addressed by a polite human face-to-face rather than a band detached from reality by a stage.

"I'm sorry," he told me in a heavy German accent, choosing his words. "I don't like Christians."

I shrugged. "Lots of people don't. How come?"

"Christians think they are world police," he said. "American Christians solve problems with bombs."

I nodded. This was fair.

He went on. "Maybe not you, but American Christian has very bad reputation here. Very bad. I am sorry."

"It's okay," I told him. "We have a bad reputation in America too."

When our plane touched down in the States a few weeks later, we had several gigs before the next break. One of them was in Georgia. I was sitting beside our merch table, falling asleep guarding an array of T-shirts, CDs, and stickers, because those were the kinds of things bands sold in those days. Some guys in camo fatigues knocked on the white plastic tabletop.

"Hey," one of them was barking. "What's up with this?"

He pointed to one of our T-shirts. There was probably an image of an inverted American flag or a smashed assault rifle or some such thing. I was tired.

"It's, uh, a reference to one of our songs," I said, rubbing my face. He didn't like this answer.

One of the other soldier guys told his friend, "You know what, forget it." He said, "The only reason they can even play in this little band and make their little shirts is because soldiers like you and me fought for their freedom."

As the two of them walked away, I could hear one of them say, "I thought this was supposed to be a Christian band."

Whether it was Vienna or Savannah, someone thought the Christians were getting their politics all wrong. Being a Christian, people kept telling me, necessitated a specific political doctrine. The Christians were vesting the credibility of their faith in right-wing ideology, while the non-Christians insisted that this was the very thing that discredited Christianity. Everywhere I went, the Christians and the non-Christians suspected me of dubious faith and their reason was the same: politics.

DECONSTRUCTING AN EMPIRE

A famously depressing study published in 2007 found that 75 percent of young non-Christians had a negative perception of Christians for being "too involved in politics."[6] I doubt this really surprised anyone. On the right side of the aisle, nervous, pearl-clutching conservatives lament their children being duped by the Left, won over by the political machine. Meanwhile, on the left side, those rebellious troublemaking kids are telling their therapists about the lingering childhood trauma of being raised by quasi-Christian Republicans.

Christians making a mess of Christianity is nothing new.

In the New Testament, Paul writes to his friend Titus saying, Look, the church in the city called Crete is going to have to change. It's going to have to prove its redemptive potential in the court of public opinion because as it is, it is making a mockery of the gospel. To accomplish this gospel takeover, Paul doesn't suggest revolt or social upheaval or lobbying or legislation. Instead, he makes simple but incredible commands about the lives of Christians and communities in Crete.

Don't hide from culture, don't reach for power to coerce the culture, but live and love in the ways of gentleness, peace, and self-sacrificial love—rejecting the corruption of the world around you. There's no culture war, and there's no assimilation into the culture. There's an entirely different way of life.

Paul writes: "Remind the people to be subject to rulers and authorities, to be obedient, to be ready to do whatever is good, to slander no one, to be peaceable and considerate, and always to be gentle toward everyone" (Titus 3:1–2).

The New Testament is peppered with commands like this one.

Americans love it because, divorced of its context, it can sound like Paul is telling modern Christians to get behind a certain political party or politician. But the New Testament wasn't written to modern

Americans. Each word was drafted in a time and place where the governing authorities were set up to persecute the Jewish people and the early Christians. Any system that stood in opposition to Roman rule (direct or indirect, practical or theoretical) must go.

And yet, we don't have any writings in the New Testament or from the early church that command "Christianizing" the empire. The empire, it turns out, is fundamentally unchristian. The early church understood that while you can try to legislate behavior, it won't reform hearts.

That can be hard for us to accept.

And it's not for no good reason that so many Christians chase after political power. We can't help but see brokenness, corruption, and evil in our world, and we want it to change. That's good. God gave us that fire. But no politician or political party encapsulates God's vision for justice and goodness. Depending on personality, preference, and upbringing, people tend to pick one and demonize the other. When I was a kid in the '80s and '90s, my parents' generation deified the Right and demonized the Left. Today, it's millennials and Gen-Zers deifying the Left and demonizing the Right.

There's no "Christian" way to do any of this.

The angry, reactionary deconstruction mentality believes that to claim Christianity is tantamount to becoming an active member of the Republican party and the NRA. They think that to cleanse Christianity of its bad reputation, we need to encourage political involvement in the other direction. But being a Christian doesn't make someone a gun-wielding right-winger any more than being a Muslim makes someone a suicide bomber, or being a vegan makes someone a pretentious jerk. (As a vegan, I'd like to think I exemplify this, but I can't bear to associate with nonvegans long enough to find out.)

These angry reactionary deconstructionists insist that God needs saving from the elephants, and the only way to rescue him is to send in the donkeys. Everyone is saying the same thing, really. It's not that they think Christianity has been corrupted by the politics of the empire. It's just been corrupted by the *wrong side*. Who the heck is the wrong side? Depends on who you ask.

A SUBURBAN FASHIONISTA
IN A METALLICA T-SHIRT

Human beings, as a general rule, are not always the best at separating bad apples from sprawling orchards. A single fiery one-star Amazon review means the product is inherently defective. We're even worse at getting past negative public perception. We wonder, Can I belong to this band's fan base? Is this movie trending? Am I still cool if I like something that is decidedly uncool? Must I pretend to like it ironically?

We wonder, What does liking this post say about me as a person?

Ambiguity is frustrating. If the world thinks Christians are the gun-toting, flag-waving, moral-policing, political zealots clearly exemplified by the bad apples, we want out of the orchard. Because what if people think we're one of *them*?

Politicized quasi Christians are like sheltered suburban fashionistas who buy Metallica T-shirts from H&M without realizing it's a band. Is this license enough for snooty metalheads to throw out their beloved copies of *Master of Puppets*, or is it that a few misguided people misrepresenting a thing doesn't necessarily corrupt the thing itself?

And really, how arrogant can you get? How flimsy was our hold on the thing we claimed to believe in the first place? Do we really imagine ourselves so superior to other imperfect people that we cannot bear the idea that these people would even pretend to belong to the same group? If a tween poser in a Metallica shirt is enough to make you disown the band, then dare I say, maybe *you* were the one who was never really a Metallica fan.

This is the irony of those deconstructing in the wake of politicized evangelicalism. They claim that so-called Christians emphasizing their right-wing politics are a burden too heavy for their fragile faith to carry. It's not Jesus's reputation being vandalized that bothers deconstructionists but a violation of *their* political ideals that does them in.

If it's Jesus you want, abandon the politics. If it's politics you want, abandon Jesus.

The deconstructionists are doing the very thing they attribute to the downfall of their belief, just on the other side of the aisle. "You don't really love Jesus," they accuse. "You only love your politics!" How do they confront this hypocrisy? By abandoning Jesus and holding fast to their politics.

Every disciple of Jesus has to face the frustrating reality of our politically divided world. Will we acknowledge the kingship of Jesus—the supremacy of it—even when it forces us beyond the boundaries of a side?

You may well have practical opinions about how government should be run. That's fine. Everyone does. You may think one policy makes more sense than another, that one politician is more capable than another, at least in the context of world government. The danger is in becoming convinced that your political opinions capture the unique *Christian* vision for justice and goodness. No political system can bear that weight, and when it begins to crumble, you'll be left struggling to stand your broken Christianity upright in the dust and debris of your political idolatry.

This happens when you become convinced that everything hangs on having your people in power and that everything will collapse if they aren't. Thinking of this kind inevitably demonizes your political opponents, creates a moral high ground based not on the teachings of Jesus but on the politics of the world, and ushers us quietly into the hateful outrage boiling up around us on all sides.

It's easier. I'll give it that.

It's easier to convince yourself every Republican is one way, or every Democrat is another way—that everything can and should be viewed through the lens of politics, that what's most important and revelatory about a person is the way they vote. That the only way to change the world is with that vote.

But then we return to this strange and subversive story of a people in the first century. The small, persecuted minority whose answer to the evils of empire and being persecuted by political power was: "Remind the people to be subject to rulers and authorities, to be obedient, to be ready to do whatever is good, to slander no one, to be peaceable and considerate, and always to be gentle toward everyone" (Titus 3:1–2).

If this does not describe the disposition of the church toward power, then we have disobeyed our king and we need to repent. There is a place for righteous indignation against evil and injustice and to take action against it. There is a place to recognize and acknowledge the evils and corruption of the state. But we belong to a different king and a different kingdom. Our methods are not of this world.

The earliest disciples of Jesus refused to participate in the political systems of their time and place. They denounced allegiance to rulers and regimes, refused to go to war for *or against* the empire—though they had every reason for the latter. They were a lonely grassroots rabble suffering routine injustice under the tyranny of the system, and they heralded a radical and subversive announcement of a new king and a new kingdom.

And yet . . .

The early church teaching on how to engage the political machine was: Pray for those in power (even though, in their context, the powerful were evil and oppressive). Love your enemies, pay taxes, and as much as they don't require you to disobey Jesus, quietly follow the rules. Do all this knowing that these earthly rulers are not your masters. Jesus is Lord. Caesar is not. Love God, love others. This, they taught, will change the world.

A kind of quiet defiance. A peaceful, spiritual revolt.

Today, the New Testament approach to political power will bring you under attack by both the right and the left sides of the aisle. Even if following Jesus puts me at odds with every political party and every governmental system on earth and across history, I will follow him forever come hell or high water.

If I am hated by the Right and the Left, and if I am forever politically homeless, I will be home in the kingdom. There's no culture war, and there's no assimilation into the culture. There's a different way of life. I live under the teachings and lordship of Jesus, not a political party or a Facebook mob, or a snarky Instagram story. I will not be led by the cultural pressure of my time and place.

I am not setting out to live my life according to social media rhetoric or because of my anger toward a politician or because I'm scared of being called privileged. I want to do what Jesus tells me to do, and if the world hates me, I will be in good company.

I want to lead a quiet life, following the rules, paying taxes, being *in* America but not *of* America.

When the world around you—especially the news media and social media, in which so many are deeply entrenched—bombards you with its unending life-and-death propaganda, it seems hard to believe that Jesus taught us to change the world in obscurity, quietly living out his commands as the family of God, the church.

But the gospel did change the world this way. And it still does.

And it still can.

The Apprentice: A Reckoning for Frauds

As the Apprentice walked with the Master, he learned to walk with other apprentices. There was always someone, several people, a crowd. This was good. When someone collapsed on the road (as was often the case), those who walked beside the felled disciple would lift them back up. When someone took a wrong turn, when they wandered from the Master's road, others would go off to find them. Sometimes they'd succeed in bringing them back. Sometimes they wouldn't. Sometimes things were bad.

These other apprentices, it seemed, snapped and snarled and clawed at one another as often as they embraced in familial love. A few of them would cloister themselves away from the group so they could whisper about the others, their words pregnant with envy and hate. Sometimes, one apprentice would shove another to the ground, and no one helped them to their feet at all. Sometimes an apprentice would wander from the road, and the others would laugh and say, Let them go. Who needs them?

Sometimes the Apprentice loved those who walked alongside him, and other times he hated them. Sometimes the Apprentice was shoved, and sometimes he did the shoving. The only reason he ever did the shoving, he told himself, is because he had been shoved first.

The ordeal of walking with others often seemed more trouble than it was worth. The Master would tell his followers to be gentle with one another, and immediately one apprentice would scream at another. The Master would tell his followers to care for one another, and one apprentice would strike another. The Master would tell his followers to serve one another, but it often seemed as though every apprentice was mostly serving themselves.

The apprentices would pass bystanders as they traveled, others who lined the road of discipleship and looked in, curious, observing. The bystanders, they would see the Master out in front, and they knew that the throng of pursuing apprentices was meant to emulate the one leading them. Sometimes the bystanders found the apprentices on a good day, but often, their collective failure was a grand, public spectacle.

The Apprentice worried maybe no one would ever understand the Master if everyone following him was always failing so miserably. He went to the Master to voice his concerns.

"Master," said the Apprentice, "these other followers of yours, I worry that they will corrupt our movement."

The Master smiled. "Ours has always been a movement for failures. Let them follow me."

"Will you overlook their disobedience?"

"I will not. I will hold them accountable. So will you. So will the others."

The Apprentice looked back at the bevy of delinquent followers and sneered. "Master," he said, "all our accountability hasn't stopped their failure."

"Nor yours," the Master said.

The Master's words hurt the Apprentice, but when he looked into the Master's face it was filled with kindness and compassion.

"Accountability does not end all failure forever," the Master said. "Accountability keeps us walking the road. It teaches us not to fail the same way."

"I wonder if some of them are insincere," the Apprentice grumbled. "I wonder if some of them are really apprentices at all."

"Some of them aren't," said the Master. "This too will be reckoned." The Master looked back at his imperfect followers, and where the Apprentice wore contempt on his face as he beheld them, the Master's face beamed with love and affection.

"They fail me. They hurt me," the Master said. "But I love them. I choose to forgive them. Maybe if you do the same, all of you will walk the road a little easier."

THE FOURTH GREAT PREDATOR: HYPOCRISY

"The truth is, cathedrals don't mean anything special to me. Nothing. Cathedrals. They're something to look at on late-night TV. That's all they are."

—RAYMOND CARVER, "CATHEDRAL"

Chapter 9

MY FATHER WAS A RACIST
AND I LOVED HIM

THE FIRST TIME I heard a racial slur, my dad was saying it. My blood went cold. My mom, hearing this from another room, rebuked my dad. I wasn't sure what I'd heard, but everything about the situation, the tone of his voice, the horror in my mom's, it was all very clear that he'd said something awful.

It was not the last time I would hear him say the word.

I was raised by a racist man in the racist culture of the small racist world of the rural Deep South. The racial demographic of my time and place was somewhere to the tune of 54 percent Black and 39 percent White. A racial tension ornamented everything like beige wallpaper, familiar to the point of invisibility. This is the world that raised and reared my father, and it was the enabling permission slip of the Southern Christian.

"They don't know any better," people would say in order to keep the racism alive rather than endure the painfully invasive surgery necessary to remove it. "It's how they were raised." As if upbringing itself were an entity that somehow operated independently of the people carrying it out. Like nobody had any choice.

In a society reeling from the noxious stink of racism wafting up from the American septic tank and clouding the surface world like a dark fog, we assume that racism is always the obvious villainy of neo-Nazis, white hoods, and alt-right trolls. Or, furious and volatile, we penalize every insensitive infraction by pinning a swastika to it, believing there is only one dimension to racism, that racism is a binary "is" or "isn't," that the fallen pop star caught on camera shouting a hateful slur is the same as David Duke, the same as Hitler.

Racism is racism, yes. Bad is bad, sure. But there are dimensions of badness.

My dad was a racist. Before he died, we had several tearful arguments over his racism, me angry, him defensive. My dad wore the racism of his upbringing like the T-shirt of an old band whose lyrics he could remember but that he didn't really listen to anymore. If you asked him why he went on wearing the shirt, he became suddenly defensive. Every now and then, in vulnerable states of anger or anxiety, he fell back on those lyrics he'd memorized. This, I told him, was evil.

When I was younger, my father's racism mostly made me furious. When I was older, it still had the power to provoke anger in me, but mostly I was grieved.

Given that I've described my dad as racist, maybe you'd imagine him as an angry Klansman who snarled at the mere sight of someone who wasn't White. Most racist people I knew weren't really like that. My father harbored no sincere political ideologies to speak of, belonged to no formal causes. He was appalled by neo-Nazis, and he condemned the Ku Klux Klan. My dad didn't deny that racism was wrong, that it was sinful. He had, like so many of us do, given himself permission to sin.

The world he knew was majority Black, and I never saw him demonstrate any cruelty or rudeness to the Black people we encountered on any given day. My dad had Black friends, men he worked with for decades. Mostly, he assumed the right to spout off racial slurs when particularly angry or to joke within hateful stereotypes. This was the racism he fostered, the sin he refused to purge.

Southern racism is more often a dark, coiling snake that sleeps nestled in the hearts of those who inherited it from their parents. The snake waits, dormant, until pain or frustration stirs it from slumber, and it goes gliding up out of the open mouths of hateful men and women. As Jesus himself taught, "For the mouth speaks what the heart is full of" (Matt. 12:34).

A double-minded man, my dad lived willfully within the confines of an evil paradox that allowed him to nurture the satanic generational evil of racism in his heart, keeping it alive but often forgetting it was there. Knowing it was wrong but refusing to really do anything about it.

My oldest friend—someone I befriended in the third grade and with whom I remain close to this day—is Black. My dad loved him, and he loved my dad. When my dad died, this friend of mine bought plane tickets immediately so that he could be at my dad's funeral. I didn't even know my friend was coming; I hadn't expected him to interrupt his life and budget in so significant a way, but then there he was. My mom held on to him, weeping, so grateful and so moved by his gesture of self-sacrificial love.

My friend knew that my dad was racist, but he also knew that no person is one thing only.

My dad was racist, but he was also one of the kindest, most generous, and self-sacrificial men I have ever known. He worked his fingers to the bone for other people, for my mom, and for our family, and even for my friends. My dad was given the curious blessing of one of the most unconventional sons that his small, Southern world had ever known, and rather than banish or denounce this strange young man—his loud music and dyed hair, the only young man with tattoos and painted black fingernails in the tri-state area—my dad loved and supported him shamelessly and without hesitation. Doing this cost him.

My dad gave time, finances, energy, his life to others. He served my family, served the church. My dad demonstrated a life of generous, disciplined faithfulness that is completely alien to my generation, and he did it with quiet gratitude.

When my dad's significant health woes were first beginning, a doctor warned him that not taking better care of himself would inevitably conclude in needlessly premature death. I overheard my dad recounting the doctor's words to my mom one evening. I heard him say, "Well, if I died tomorrow, it's been a good life."

I remember wondering what he meant. To my ambitious teenage mind, my dad's life seemed uneventful. Me? I wanted to do things. I wanted to travel the world, make art, achieve some illusory notion of lasting significance. I wanted to matter. But my dad? He'd worked at a paper mill his entire adult life. He lived on a dirt road and cared for a family. He spent most of his time doing things for other people. He dedicated much of my adolescence and early adulthood to pouring resources into my ambition to pursue my vision of becoming a poor, itinerant punk rock musician despite ridicule and condemnation from friends, family, and peers.

My dad opened his home to an unending host of touring bands with whom we traveled for many years, inviting strangers from around the world to his table, preparing meals for them. I asked him once if he felt inconvenienced by this, and he told me he felt grateful. Hearing stories of the way my brother and I had been cared for in our travels, he told me that if strangers around the world invited his sons into their homes, he would do the same. My dad told me that knowing there were kind people all over the world who had been generous and caring to my brother and me in our travels had inspired him to become the same kind of person for other people's kids.

My dad was kind, generous, disciplined, self-sacrificial, and racist. I am convinced that all of us are, in our own ways, like my dad. He could be short-tempered, cruel, prideful, stubborn, unrepentant, and he could be caring, wise, and self-effacing. He wasn't one thing or the other. He was all of them. I loved my dad.

FEELING YOURSELF DISINTEGRATE

I began therapy in the winter. I was not doing well. My wife and I were living in Portland during one of the snowiest seasons in the city's history. My lifelong on-again, off-again battle against self-loathing and despair had reached a fever pitch. My interior world was becoming dominated by such unbearable darkness that I was worried about what might happen if nothing changed. Like my father before me, I'd carried the dark doppelgänger within, content to bear the unforgiving burden of hatred. One afternoon on a cold city sidewalk, I told my friend Bethany that I'd made my first appointment with a therapist, and I watched the words leave me like gray clouds in the cold. Bethany knew I wasn't doing great. She smiled in a way I didn't understand then but do now and told me she was proud of me.

I wasn't. I don't think I felt a single positive thing about myself.

All this I explained to my therapist during our first conversation, and we talked about it then, and the next week, and the next, until the weeks became months, became years.

It took a long time and a lot of resources and work, but that once volatile struggle against self-loathing and despair eventually became less so. Then it became peripheral, then distant—and through that work in therapy, in prayer, in spiritual formation and community, and because of the healing kindness of God, it became mostly a memory. This required years of work, and the work was not seamless.

Self-loathing is evil. A sin no different than hating a brother or sister who is created in the image of God. Self-loathing and despair are nefarious sins because they masquerade as humility but are, in reality, deeply self-obsessed. They sabotage relationships, cripple spiritual formation, stifle maturity—to put it plainly, they, like all sin, rob you of life.

Today, in this season of my life, I don't struggle with self-loathing. I'm aware of my own shortcomings, but I genuinely like myself. I don't lapse arbitrarily into the nihilistic pit of hopelessness. I sometimes get frustrated or pessimistic or melancholy like anyone else with the same bent, but I am better equipped to navigate these emotions without being seized by the horrible black claws of despair.

To overcome a particular cyclical pattern of destructive behavior, to feel the freeing joy of repentance (when you turn from one path and walk a new one instead) and the freedom it affords is intoxicating. It's like realizing what clean water tastes like after years of drinking from a gutter. Intimacy between God and myself was unclouded, discipline came easier, my focus was sharpened. Without the heavy burden of failure chained to my back, I walked gratefully upright.

Until I messed something else up.

I was telling my therapist all of this a couple dozen meetings in, gearing up to ask a very important question. How is it, I asked him, that after all this work and breakthrough, how is it that some new failure manages to find me?

Some new struggle. Some new mode of an old screw-up.

In spiritual formation, we sometimes use the term "integration" to describe what happens to the disciple of Jesus as they mature in faithful obedience, as they experience more freedom, more peace. Wasn't I becoming more integrated? I asked my therapist. I'm sure I was. How is it then that some new sin besets me, and I feel as if I was never really integrated at all? He smiled and opened a drawer in his desk, drawing from it a printed article he'd kept for teaching moments like this one.

"Josh," he said, "did you know that Brennan Manning lived in New Orleans during Hurricane Katrina?"

Brennan Manning was an author I'd read for years. His writing hadn't just been massively formational for me. It had been healing for my soul. But I didn't really know where he lived or when he lived there.

"After the storm," my therapist said, "Brennan Manning got a call from *Christianity Today*, who interviewed him, wanting his take on the chaos unfolding in New Orleans."

My therapist looked at the article, saying, "He, Manning, is predictably humble and self-effacing, but he told the magazine that he'd remained in the city even after the storm set in so that he could help others. He said that he'd helped identify lost children, helped an old woman find a ride out of town."

That sounded like a nice, Jesusy thing to do.

"But," my therapist interrupted himself, looking up from the paper, "a few days after the article went to press, Brennan Manning called the offices of *Christianity Today* to clarify one important detail of his story."

The clarification appears as an editor's note at the article's heading, and my therapist read it aloud that morning:

> From the Editors: We regret to inform our readers that, following this on-the-record conversation, Brennan Manning called our office to apologize. He reiterated that he had been "disoriented, confused, and depressed" lately and that certain details he provided were not true. He did not help identify a child from his apartment complex. He did not help an elderly woman get a ride. And while he was the last one to leave his apartment complex, "the truth is that there was nobody around here for me to help," he said in a voice message to *Christianity Today*. "The essential truth: I lied."[1]

When he'd finished reading this to me, my therapist was still smiling. I was about to understand something crucial about following Jesus.

Chapter 10

BROOD OF VIPERS

THE POLICEMAN'S FLASHLIGHT HURT my eyes. I don't know why they do this, cops. I was squinting into the blinding white beam of the flashlight through the open window of my 1984 Ford Aerostar.

"You been drinking?" the cop asked in a Georgian drawl.

"No, sir," I answered. As a Southerner, I'd been raised to address all elders and strangers as either "sir" or "ma'am."

My eyes darted to his nameplate. This kind of thing happened all the time, so I'd learned to remember names.

"Out of the vehicle," he said.

Standing on the side of the road, the light was still in my eyes.

"Are you male or female?" he asked me.

"Male."

He shrugged, making a big theatrical show of his surprise. "I couldn't tell."

He moved the flashlight to the side of my head. "Do you think you're tough with those safety pins in your ears?" he asked.

"Not really."

"If I had a faggot like you for a son, I'd snatch that little earring right out of his lip."

I didn't say anything. What could I say?

"What am I going to find if I search the van?" he asked.

"Nothing. Some trash. CDs."

"Put your hands on the hood of the vehicle."

He walked me to the front of the van and forced me down over the hood, kicking my legs to make space and grabbing at my jeans in search of, what? A weapon? I stayed like this, bent over the hood, while the officer tore the insides of my van apart.

"There is a dry, leafy substance in the ashtray!" he shouted from inside the van.

I had no idea what he was talking about. Dirt, maybe? I lifted my hands from the hood and inched forward. The cop whirled around, drawing his gun and leveling it at me.

"Put your hands back on that hood *right now!*"

I returned to the hood, the gun on me as I went.

By the time the officer had completed his "investigation," he'd emptied my CD book into the passenger seat and torn my glove-box door from the hinges.

He asked me again how much alcohol was in my system (none), what drugs I'd taken (zilch), what kind of illicit shenanigans I'd been up to (watching a movie with a friend). He leaned in close, sneering, told me that he knew I was a liar and that I was lucky I wouldn't be going to jail that night.

The next morning, I told my friend about the incident. As I described the cop, my friend furrowed his brows. He asked the officer's name. When he heard it, my friend laughed.

"Oh, yeah. He's a deacon at my church."

BEHOLD, THE MONKEY

Sometime in the 1930s, Elías García Martínez painted a portrait of Jesus on the wall at Sanctuary of Mercy church in Borja, Spain. The painting is a fresco called *Ecce Hommo* (Latin for "Behold the Man"), an unremarkable representation of Jesus looking forlorn beneath his crown of thorns. As the decades marched on, the paint flaked from the plaster wall, a white, creeping erasure making its way up Jesus's robe, eating a void in his face.

Eventually, elderly parishioner Cecilia Giménez decided to do something before the painting deteriorated to nothing. Cecilia wasn't an artist and had no experience with portraits or frescos, but she figured, Hey, how hard can it be? Her "restoration" features a bulbous ape-like monstrosity leering from cold dead shark eyes fixed on a crooked mask wreathed in brown fur. The effort was so hilariously bad that in 2012, it became a global comedy phenomenon that proliferated on social media and via news coverage, eventually earning its own title, *Ecce Mono* ("Behold the Monkey").

This, to me, is about as good a metaphor for humanity as any.

We were created with intention and purpose, made very good, but we've been worn down and whittled away. Attempting to restore ourselves, to put back what's missing, we've been twisted, corrupted, broken and bent out of shape by our own selfishness and the horrors of an evil-infested nightmare world.

We don't look much like what was intended, but we're in there somewhere. It's the same painting beneath all the disfiguring gunk, the scrapes and erosion and time.

A RAPIST AFTER GOD'S OWN HEART

If you've spent time in the company of Christians, you've likely heard of King David, "a man after God's own heart" (see 1 Sam. 13:14; Acts 13:22). This man after God's heart, this hero of the Bible, infamously ogled a bathing woman, Bathsheba. The hero-king knows Bathsheba is married, but he uses his kingly power to send for her and have sex with her. (Many argue that David raped Bathsheba.)[1,2] She gets pregnant. Rather than dealing with the fallout of his evil, the hero king persists in it, manipulating his subjects and military strategy to have Bathsheba's husband killed, then bringing his grieving widow into the corruption of David's polygamy. Abused, violated, widowed by murder, Bathsheba becomes one among David's many wives and concubines.

Cover to cover, the Bible's story uniformly condemns everything David does in this story with severe contempt.

Later in the Bible, there's a song that David wrote about his grief over the incident. This song, written by a murdering sexual predator, is beautiful. In it, David summarizes one of the Bible's more dire concepts with poetic brevity: "Surely I was sinful at birth, sinful from the time my mother conceived me. Yet you desired faithfulness even in the womb" (see Psalm 51).

God wants what God can't get: faithfulness from screw-ups.

A newborn or a fetus can't really do anything "sinful." The point of this lyrical hyperbole is that people—all people—have a selfish bent. We tend to think of children as innocent, but the "innocence" of children is over with as soon as they can see more than a few feet in front of them. Kids learn selfishness without being taught. Even children smothered in affectionate generosity from birth learn from an early age to shout, "Mine!" Most human beings go on shouting this, on some level, until they die.

All of us are, on some level, not so great.

Like so many others, I have been deeply inspired by the life and teaching of Dr. Martin Luther King Jr. His commitment to the teachings of Jesus, his inarguable mastery of preaching, and his relentless passion for nonviolence have significantly impacted my vocation and discipleship. And I always knew that Dr. King had been accused of frequent unfaithfulness to his wife.

The extramarital affairs of Martin Luther King Jr. have been well publicized for decades. Depending on which source you read, the sorts of things Dr. King was accused of range from hypocritical and destructive to heinous, criminal evil. I wasn't there, so I have no idea what really happened. But I wouldn't be surprised if some or all of it were true. Not because I have a dismal view of Dr. King's character, but because I have a dismal view of humanity itself.

In his stand-up special, *The Age of Spin,* Dave Chapelle explained this universal paradox of human good and evil using Bill Cosby as an archetype. After Cosby was accused of and then convicted for a litany of sexual crimes, fans of Cosby's comedy and philanthropy were left to grapple with the reality of good and evil in tension within the same man.

"He partnered up with a clinical psychologist to make sure that there was not one negative image of African Americans on his show," Chapelle told his audience. "That's no small thing. He gave tens of millions of dollars to African American institutions of higher learning and is directly responsible for thousands of Black kids going to college." Thus, Chapelle confessed, "He has a valuable legacy that I can't just throw away."[3]

Good and evil in the same place. In the same man.

In the hyperpartisan dystopia of the posttruth Western civilization, we've dispensed with the tension and ambiguity of the human condition, creating political opponents of the world and dismissing them with unthinking blanket statements. The 2020 plague era became the season of dichotomy, of crushing people into accommodating cubes and filing them into binary categories. Racists and antiracists. Liberals and conservatives. White supremacists and social justice warriors. Protestors and counterprotestors. Democrats and Republicans. Misogynists and feminists. Gay. Straight. Queer. Cis.

Something for everyone to hate. Demonizing strangers behind the cowardly mask of a smartphone.

In black-and-white legalist groupthink, Dr. King's civil rights achievements are nullified by his affairs, or his affairs are nullified by his civil rights achievements. In all or nothing cancel culture moralism, Bill Cosby is reduced to his crimes against women, effectively erasing his artistic and humanitarian contributions from history. In cancel culture legalism, to acknowledge the tension between Cosby's good and Cosby's evil—to acknowledge Cosby's good *at all*—is akin to endorsing his evil.

Nobody wants to endorse Bill Cosby.

Nobody wants to fraternize with the enemy, whoever the heck the enemy is to them. To a conservative, being accused of liberalism is unbearable. To a Democrat, "Republican" is a four-letter word. In either camp, it's *everyone else* who's the problem. As far as I can tell, just about everyone is pretty awful from time to time.

THE WORLD IS (NOT) A FINE PLACE

In David Fincher's neo-noir masterpiece *Se7en*, the film's only line of voice-over is delivered by William Somerset. Having witnessed such overwhelming and ugly brutality in his career as a homicide detective, Somerset tells the viewer: "Ernest Hemingway once wrote, 'The world is a fine place and worth fighting for.' I agree with the second part."[4]

I wonder why Somerset agrees with the second part. It's not that I disagree, per se, but it's a tough question to answer. Why would anyone think the world is worth fighting for? As someone who seeks out and obsesses over the gory details of the world's evil underbelly, I can't help but feel a bit cynical sometimes. For every wave of national outrage over a single incident of evil or injustice, I think of a few dozen more that Twitter missed. I think of the weeping toddler caught on camera in some department store, confused and tugging at the limp arm of her unconscious junky mom who passed out in the cereal aisle. I think of the tiny victims of notorious child murderer Albert Fish.

Over the years, I've wandered into and internalized stories like these, and it was stories like these that eroded my baseline belief in human goodness, the belief with which most of us are born. I wasn't a happy optimist shouting from the rooftops about human goodness or anything, but I think most of us take for granted a basic human decency that we kind of need in order to operate in society.

Most people don't go around arguing their belief in human decency, but you can see their need for this belief to endure in their unwillingness to inconvenience themselves with stories of unimaginable horror that unfold every day of the long calendar year. These stories needle the protective bubble of our comfortable world, and we need the bubble. If something truly depraved happens, we'd rather not know about it unless it's packaged as entertainment, a true-crime podcast, or a Netflix docuseries.

But there have been days when some awful and true story finds me, and I remember certain moments, sitting back in my chair and praying, "My God, . . . how can you love a world like this?"

God's anger conflicts us. Squinting at problematic Bible stories with our trauma and parent wounds, we want someone to come along and tidy these embarrassing passages from the page. But I can tell you that when I read about the crimes that undo my baseline belief in human goodness, I feel a number of things. I feel heartbroken, deeply grieved, seized by sadness.

And I feel furious.

Not a rage directed at villains and victimizers only, but a wave of profound anger against evil itself.

And I imagine how God must feel.

Thousands of years ago, the prophet Isaiah lamented:

> All of us have become like one who is unclean,
>   and all our righteous acts are like filthy rags;
>
> we all shrivel up like a leaf,
>   and like the wind our sins sweep us away.
>
> No one calls on your name
>   or strives to lay hold of you;
>
> for you have hidden your face from us
>   and have given us over to our sins. (Isa. 64:6–7)

And the centuries rolled on to the tune of war, human trafficking, and global warming. Behind the heavy curtain of toxic smog billowing from industrial smokestacks lies a smoldering and decimated natural world, where child slaves pick cotton to make T-shirts and tennis shoes. Where terrified animals are dragged screaming from their mothers at birth, packed into filthy pens by the thousands, pumped full of drugs, and tortured as factory farms dump rivers of industrial sludge into rural wastelands, so we can stay sick and slow and full of ninety-nine cent hamburgers.

Eyes glazed over, faces lit by the dull electric glow of a touch screen, commodified by clicks and follows to be bought and sold by corporations as minutes, hours, days, and weeks of our lives fall from the calendar, one ignored Screen Time report after another.

And a year finds us wide-eyed and unprepared as viral sickness sweeps the face of the earth, bringing with it political discord, civil unrest, the misinformation campaign of political megalomaniacs on the Right and the Left, playing their crooked flutes for angry mobs forming long lines behind them.

And every day, the for-profit news industry drip-feeds outrage hysteria to clamoring customers: more violence, racism, police brutality, wildfires, unbreathable smoke, protests, riots. The only things stopping near-daily mass shootings were quarantine and lockdown.

And as angry Americans take to social media to broadcast meltdowns, elsewhere in the world, someone else is killed. Elsewhere in the world, a homeless mother huddles with her shivering toddler on a wet and freezing street corner as people pass, oblivious and uncaring, and the toddler wakes to find her mother stiff and cold. Elsewhere in the world, another priest extends his shaking, furious hands over another casket, even smaller than the last one, and he asks—in keeping with the psalmists of centuries prior—*Is the good Lord deaf?*

All of this thanks to *people.*

It seems as if many people take for granted that evil is something that happens beyond themselves, almost entirely without, and rarely, if ever, within. There *are* terrible people in the world, such a person concedes, and surely there are fantastic hypocrites and undeniable phonies. But our imaginary person concludes, whoever these evil hypocrites are, I'm not one of them.

I once attended an event hosted on the International Day for the Elimination of Violence against Women. The speaker was passionate and inspiring, her speech eye-opening. She was also wearing a sweater by H&M and sneakers by Nike. The Global Slavery Index estimates that among the 40 million people living in modern slavery today, women represent the overwhelming majority, working in the supply chains of Western clothing brands. I have no doubt that the woman speaking that morning stirred many to action with her profound and convicting message of truth. But she delivered her message decked out in fast fashion, knowingly or unknowingly participating in the abuse and enslavement of women around the world.

Good and evil in the same place, a thin haze of hypocrisy moving through everything like water.

We like to think that evil nullifies good, that hypocrisy always exposes the absolute insincerity of any good thing a person ever did. Maybe sometimes it does, but most of the time, it confirms what, deep down, we already know. People can accomplish very good and very evil things in the same lifetime.

A mind-boggling number of noteworthy Christians have been exposed for their breathtaking hypocrisy. Sometimes, I'm sure, the moral failure, the crime, the affair, the abuse, the scandal, the suicide, indicates that the exposed hypocrite was not, in reality, an authentic disciple of Jesus. Other times, the exposure serves to remind us of the unfortunate reality of the human condition.

Christians, like all humans, can be hypocrites.

RELIEVED BY DEATH

The widow sat weeping beside me. I asked if she'd like to talk, but really, I didn't presume to have any soothing words of wisdom for someone in the throes of agonizing loss. When she spoke up, she surprised me.

"Really, what I feel is relief," she said through her tears.

She'd loved her husband deeply, and he had, in many ways, been a good man. He also menaced her with years of dehumanizing verbal abuse. He'd kept her in terror, brandished a gun at her, threatened her life. Everyone else, they knew only the good man. They'd been celebrating him, memorializing him, lamenting his death. But the widow, she somehow carried sorrow and secret relief in the same shaking body as she sat weeping beside me. She'd loved her husband, but having a constant parade of sympathizers celebrate his goodness, with all her years of unaddressed trauma, was tearing her apart.

"How can a person know Jesus and do these things?" she asked. Maybe she was asking me, maybe she was asking God. Then, turning to me for the first time, she said, "I didn't want him to die. I loved him. But am I a monster for being relieved that he's gone?"

These are the knots of our brokenness. A man tormented by his own evil who leaves his widowed wife tormented by the sense of both grief and solace crowded within her.

Jesus's disciple Peter was a hypocrite. Peter often exemplifies the paradox of our coexisting brokenness and sanctification. In the biographies of Jesus's life, Peter plays both the hero and the fool. Jesus bestows upon Peter the honor of being called the rock on which Jesus will build his movement. And he did! Today, the movement of Jesus thrives across the known world, built on Peter's confession that Jesus was who he claimed to be. All Christians belong to this heritage.

But Jesus also rebuked Peter by calling him Satan.

Get behind me, Satan.

And sadly, all disciples of Jesus follow Peter in this heritage as well. This is the tragedy of our cycles of integration and disintegration.

I remember what my therapist told me about Brennan Manning. I sat in his office that winter reading the editor's note in *Christianity Today* a second time.

> We regret to inform our readers that, following this on-the-record conversation, Brennan Manning called our office to apologize. He reiterated that he had been "disoriented, confused, and depressed" lately and that certain details he provided were not true.[5]

Nearing the end of his life, having written best-selling books and traveled abroad speaking to innumerable churches and conferences, a sought-after pastoral personality and theological mind, Manning had followed Jesus for decades. And here he was, "disoriented, confused, and depressed."

And he lied.

My therapist—a PhD, psychologist of many years, and also a follower of Jesus—said: "Josh, this side of resurrection, none of us become fully integrated and stay that way. Instead, we go through cycles of integration and disintegration." He continued: "Hopefully, we learn, we don't always become disintegrated in the same way. Hopefully, we don't *stay* disintegrated. But we come together, and we come apart."

This is, I have learned, neither pessimism nor fatalism. It is the way of the broken world and the broken people in it. Why did Brennan Manning devote his life to writing and teaching the things of Jesus? Because he loved the Master. Because he believed in him.

But how did he become an alcoholic? Get divorced? Why did he fabricate little heroisms to impress *Christianity Today*? Why did he lie?

Because he was a human being. Broken. Earlier in his life, Manning himself wrote this:

> There is a myth flourishing in the church today that has caused incalculable harm: once converted, fully converted. In other words, once I accept Jesus Christ as my Lord and Savior, an irreversible, sinless future beckons. Discipleship will be an untarnished success story; life will be an unbroken upward spiral toward holiness. Tell that to poor Peter who, after three times professing his love for Jesus on the beach and after receiving the fullness of the Spirit at Pentecost, was still jealous of Paul's apostolic success. Often I have been asked, 'Brennan, how is it possible that you became an alcoholic after you got saved?' It is possible because I got battered and bruised by loneliness and failure; because I got discouraged, uncertain, guilt-ridden, and took my eyes off Jesus. Because the Christ-encounter did not transfigure me into an angel. Because justification by

grace through faith means I have been set in right relationship with God, not made the equivalent of a patient ether-
ized on a table.[6]

Manning was being made whole—*saved*—over the years of his life,
but never arriving on the pristine shores of sinlessness, at least not
this side of resurrection. Integrated, then disintegrated. One minute
the rock, the next minute Satan.

I thought of Mother Teresa, one of the great heroes of church history. Mother Teresa asked that, upon her death, all of her private
writings be destroyed. Instead, they were published. The public was
shocked to discover this great figure of the faith had privately wres-
tled with doubt and despair for decades. She wrote in her diary:

> There is so much deep contradiction in my soul. Such deep
> longing for God—so deep that it is painful—a suffer-
> ing continual—and yet not wanted by God—repulsed—
> empty—no faith—no love—no zeal. Souls hold no
> attraction—heaven means nothing—to me it looks like an
> empty place—the thought of it means nothing to me and
> yet this torturing longing for God. Pray for me please that
> I keep smiling at Him in spite of everything. For I am only
> His.[7]

Upon reading this, many dismissed Mother Teresa as a fraud, a
phony. But I remember reading these words and thinking, *she sounds
like a Christian.*

WORTHY OF LOVE(?)

One fall, someone went around my neighborhood erecting little
signs inscribed with the popular and ubiquitous catchphrases of the
Instagram generation like, "You are enough," and "You are worthy
of love!" I'd pass these signs on afternoon walks and think, Is that
so? Not in a woe-is-me-no-one-loves-me-I'm-so-goth kind of way,
but is anyone really worthy of love?

I believe we are loved, but is it because we are *worthy* of it? If we are
worthy of love and God loves us, then the whole grace thing is not so
amazing, not so scandalous, not really costly at all. It's just cause and

effect: we deserve to be loved, so God does it. Fair is fair. God's love for us would be more or less what we are owed. But if we are unworthy of love and yet cherished to the degree that the all-powerful, perfect, cosmic Creator and ruler of the universe would demonstrate his love in life and death, such a thing scandalizes the imagination.

If the Bible's depiction of humanity as a paradoxical tangle of concurrent good and evil is accurate, if our universal human experience of the same thing is reliable, then there's not much reason to clutch our pearls and wring our hands over the inevitability of human failure.

In May of 2021, more than a year into the coronavirus pandemic, one of my creative heroes described the way he'd been discouraged by humanity throughout the chaos of the previous year. "There was bad news that no one was mature enough to accept and rationally deal with," he said. "We as a species are too . . . stupid to band together."[8]

I thought it was interesting the way he said "we." Most of the people I knew facing a similar discouragement didn't think of the predicament in "we" terms. A few days after I'd listened to the interview, I saw someone handing out bracelets inscribed with the proud declaration, "I've been vaccinated!" As people happily received the bracelets, I heard the person distributing them say, "This way, we can tell who the good people are."

This is, in my experience, the more popular way to understand the mess we're in. It's not that humanity is bad. It's that some *other* humans are bad. Emotional health and spiritual maturity ask us to see our own brokenness reflecting in the evil of others.

I don't believe the Instagram philosophy of worthiness is actually true. I don't believe that we are worthy and beautiful exactly as we are, contrary to the popular verbiage. I believe we are God's creative masterwork, made in God's image, and in that sense we are innately beautiful. But our beauty has been marred and corrupted by our awfulness—the selfishness within that enables us to treat one another and the rest of creation without love or grace or kindness.

Nurturing long-term anger, resentment, and bitterness over the rampant failure of so-called Christians drives the furious, hurting soul further inward over time. Mad at their parents, the church that raised them, and the Christianity of their upbringing, the discontent former Christian draws a convenient floodlight on the failure of everyone else, blinding the embittered to their own failure and inconsistency. I see in innumerable deconstructing Christians a purported desire to rebel against their mom and dad, rebel against their Christian culture, rebel against the god of the evangelicals.

This isn't rebellion. It's spite.

This isn't revolution. It's a tantrum.

Sure, it would take an incredible amount of deceit or delusion to argue that Christians, throughout their long history, have not been guilty of many heinous evils in both the collective and individual sense. These evils—everything from the Crusades to Manifest Destiny to embezzlement and celebrity megachurch sex scandals—are inexcusable, objective failures to uphold and obey the teachings of Jesus and the writings of Scripture. These failures reveal humanity's deep-seated and destructive selfishness, that we are bent toward a primal sense of self-gratification and self-preservation that ironically results in self-destruction.

And all of us, Christian or otherwise, do this.

From what I can tell, some people were pretty ticked that Brennan Manning would lie about his experiences during Hurricane Katrina, and the embarrassing controversy of it can easily obscure something that might be the most important detail in the story.

The editor's note that broke the bad news of Manning's ruse read, "We regret to inform our readers that, following this on-the-record conversation, Brennan Manning called our office to apologize."

There's a story in the Bible in which Peter, the beloved disciple on whom Jesus builds his movement, denies knowing Jesus at all. He insists on denying Jesus, on denouncing him. He does it again and again, calling down curses, contending, *I don't know the man*. Later, Peter would come face-to-face with the Jesus he so emphatically denounced, and he would tell Jesus, "I love you." Peter confessed Jesus, then denied him, then confessed him again. To have been elevated by Jesus as "the rock," only to fail him in such grand spectacle, was it agonizing to stand in Jesus's presence again, having failed him so?

Doesn't anyone who follows Jesus know it to be so?

We know from early church writings that Peter, like Jesus, was crucified by Rome. But unlike Jesus, Peter was hung head down on the cross, at his own behest. Jerome, a fourth-century priest, wrote that

> at Nero's hands Peter received the crown of martyrdom being nailed to the cross with his head towards the ground and his feet raised on high, asserting that he was unworthy to be crucified in the same manner as his Lord.[9]

The disciple who once denied Jesus, the disciple who once sank in the turbulent sea when his fear was greater than his faith, would become the disciple who asked to be hung upside down because he was unworthy to die like Jesus.

Integrated, disintegrated, then integrated again.

Mr. Manning told the truth, then lied, then told the truth again. I can't say for sure, but I believe it was likely possible that the readers of *Christianity Today* might not have ever known Manning was lying had he not told them so. Why did he call? Why did he confess? Wasn't this editor's note humiliating?

Mother Teresa continued her work of caring and advocating for the sick and the poor, sharing the gospel, proclaiming the kingdom throughout the years of her quiet suffering, doubt, and despair. Why? Because the whole thing was a charade, and her pride insisted she maintain the act? Or were all these things cycles? Integration, to disintegration, then integration again through the crucible of repentance.

The story of Peter's spectacular failure is included in the Bible for the reader's sake. Aren't we like this incompetent disciple, Peter? Can we not see ourselves in him? And isn't this reflection truly dreadful to behold? That we might look upon our own awful countenance, our faces twisted, calling down curses, *I don't know the man.*

Hasn't this been us in the little lies, bitter words, and selfish secrets? Hasn't this been us in our thoughtless hoarding and consumption of money and resources, our overlooking the poor, our prioritizing our own comfort and desire over the world's pain? Hasn't this been us in our denying our friends, spouses, and children time and relational energy that we devote to devices and screens while they wait, abandoned and longing for our hearts and attention while we drain both into smartphones and streaming services?

I don't know the man.

Hasn't this been us in our shopping and excess? In demanding our own way? Hasn't this been every Christian the millions of times we've taken the easy road in the name of laziness and cowardice when Jesus beckoned us plainly down the difficult road that leads to life? Jesus wants obedience. We want to sleep in.

I don't know the man.

And haven't many of those same failed Christians also known what it means to drag themselves before the Jesus we denied, bedraggled and shamed by the toll of our failure, and ask him through shivering tears to receive us again?

Haven't most of us also come before him numb and at a loss for words to describe the same stupid blunder, the same ridiculous mistake, and where we could no longer muster tearful contrition before him, he saw in us a willing spirit beneath a weak flesh—and he forgave us just the same?

And somewhere, someone hated us for it. Someone could not do what God did: release us from the crushing weight of our own ineptitude and failure.

VOLUNTARY VENOM

The story of human inadequacy is plastered throughout the Bible for you and me. To read and read again. To break our hearts and steady our discipleship—from integration to disintegration to integration again, through the crucible of repentance.

The Great Predator of hypocrisy feeds on reactions. To get them, it bites, and the bite is venomous. We have little say about whether the bite hurts or whether it wounds us, but the venom's toxicity is determined by the person bitten. In my years of therapy, self-examination, and spiritual formation, I have learned that I tend to take things personally. I can be self-focused, even self-obsessed. Left to my own devices, I make things about me, including the failure of other people.

There was a time in my life when I was so thoroughly repulsed by the shameless hypocrisy of Christian culture that I refused to have any place among their ranks. I had been treated poorly by many Christians in my life, and I was hurting, angry, and bitter. I thought of those patronizing Southern men, those unashamed racists. The nationalistic frauds who clapped me on the back and patronized me with their holy concern when their lives demonstrated absolutely no evidence of the radical discipleship depicted in the Bible they used to clobber me. I thought of the Jerry Falwells, the bloodthirsty patriots, the unthinking conservatism that bludgeoned me with its Frankenstein sermons of "military violence good, rock music bad!"

In fairness, there had been Christians who, though imperfect, had represented Jesus in my life. I allowed the venom of hypocrisy to poison my senses so that I saw everything through the dark lenses of cynicism. Everyone was a charlatan, a phony, an actor. Everyone, that is, except me.

I didn't just want out. I wanted to burn the whole thing down. If you'd asked me then, I would have told you I wasn't hurt, just angry. I would have made with the theatrics, a lot of flowery talk about how I'd become wise to the con. I would have said I'd "studied" things, which meant I'd thought things over on my own, with no one else speaking into the process.

I told myself and everyone else that I didn't care what anybody thought. Admitting that I'd been hurt would give me away. I could be angry about things beyond myself, but being hurt would mean that I cared about the way I'd been treated, that I cared about the way older men and women in my life had failed to bless and encourage and lead me in self-sacrificial love.

The old wisdom about being most angry with your own reflection was, in my case, a resounding *bingo*. I had seen in the stories of Jesus a beautiful radicalism, and the domesticated civil religion of American evangelicalism had not only confirmed my fears that the so-called disciples of this romantic and radical way of life were inauthentic tourists, but that I was too.

I was sitting in the back of the dojo, waiting to see a perfect black belt. The only reason I wasn't training myself, I reasoned, was because the classes were corrupt. The sensei wasn't a master. This idle corner became a comfortable place from which to issue my gripes with everything.

I saw a lot of bad in the world and the people in it. Also, I saw a lot of bad in me, but I took comfort in knowing I was at least better than those awful pseudo-Christians. If there was some authentic Christianity, I would find it my own way, without the inherently corrupt institutions of the church and the hypocrites who populated it. I put a lot of work into focusing my attention on the failure of everyone else until it threatened to destroy me.

I spent years suspicious of all organized modes of Christianity—anything that didn't pass my test of incredible radicalism (a test I couldn't pass myself)—so that I felt itchy around anything "churchy." I liked myself less and less until I loathed myself with such fiery intensity that I wanted myself destroyed. My steady diet of venom had so twisted my insides that I could no longer find any line of delineation between myself and my failure.

An inner voice haunted me. More than an internal critic nitpicking my imperfections, the voice berated me with seething animosity. I was, like all self-loathers, deeply self-obsessed. I tracked my own movements, studied my own words, thought of myself as a distinct and contemptible other person. I hated nothing in all my life the way I have hated this person. I loathed him with such wild, unbridled intensity that I have wanted to do him harm—and often I did.

The shadowy voice of self-hatred followed me, sat on my shoulder—a vile parrot—and whispered in my ears. He grew to mammoth proportions, bigger than me, and operated me like a marionette.

If I released myself from the bonds of my enmity, I knew the prison of bitterness and cynicism I had used to entomb hordes of fraudulent, hypocritical Christians would come undone. Forgiving hypocrites meant forgiving me. Worse still, releasing myself from the awful confines of my self-loathing would become an obligation to release everyone else, to admit that whatever was wrong with everyone else was wrong with me too, and maybe all my cynicism had really done was make me miserable.

I was further from the authenticity of Jesus than ever before.

It had been a decade of bad blood, hurt feelings, and evolving belief. Then I went back to church.

I'M PRETTY SURE

One truly unbearable wrinkle in the face of conservative Christian hypocrisy is the pride of certainty. "Christians," you'll hear the deconstructionist say, "refuse to admit when they could be wrong." This is often true. For the first couple of decades of my life, the Christian culture I knew was almost entirely closed off to questions, wrestling, and doubt. It was a culture that prided itself on its own certainty, which it mistook for faith. But faith is a decision to believe in the face of uncertainty. Faith requires doubt.

Doubt is a wonderfully reassuring component of the Christian tradition. Ever since Jesus's close friends witnessed him risen from the dead—a moment when "they worshipped him; but some doubted" (Matt. 28:17)—worship and doubt have lived in the same place, and that place is the church. In the first story of worship and doubt intermingled before the risen Jesus, how did Jesus respond? By sending them out on the mission that changed the world.

These worshipping/doubting disciples, just eleven of them, who, prior to seeing Jesus resurrected from the dead, had all failed him in spectacular fashion. They'd abandoned him, denied knowing him, denounced him. Then, when their Master was vindicated, when he stood before them, having risen exactly like he said he would, they had their doubts.

If I were Jesus, I would have been frustrated. Doubt? Are you kidding? *Now?* But Jesus said to these failed, doubting apprentices: I have a job for you.

It seems as if the Christian movement often forgets its proud heritage of failure and doubt—a heritage that should release us from the agony and illusion and pridefulness of certainty. To choose to believe something is one thing. To learn and grow in wisdom is one thing. To test what you choose to believe, to learn how to explain your decision and why you continue to make it, all of this is very good. And all of this can be done without the arrogance and pretense of certainty.

But when the church insists on "I know" rather than "I believe," they tend to fashion "I know" into an ugly stick they use to clobber anyone with questions and doubts. Frustrated and injured by the certainty club, the deconstruction movement promises the freedom of ambiguity, but really, it's a bait and switch. Deconstruction promises a more progressive take on spirituality, the undoing of all those oh-so-icky dogmas of the politicized conservative fundamentalist zealots.

One beloved mantra of the progressive camp is the promise of being "on the right side of history." This, to me, is a pretty bold claim. Who thinks they're on the *wrong* side of history, really? Like soldiers at war, everyone thinks they're on the right side. Maybe for the people who so cherish being on the right side of history, they'd argue that they can make so bold a claim based on what we've learned from history itself. But it seems to me that one lesson history teaches with unequivocal reliability is that we're wrong all the time. We're wrong about science, antiquity, politics, humans, plants, animals, you name it.

But we also learn from being wrong, or at least from admitting that we are. We learn a lot on the way to our wrong ideas, and we learn even more when we confront them and move on. Some great ways to ensure very little learning happens is either by laboring under the delusion that we can never really know anything, insisting on the contradiction of intentional ambiguity, or by digging in our heels and promising that we finally figured things out *this time*.

This time we're for sure right.

Maybe a better way is to believe things. We test the things we believe. The trouble with this is that it takes a long time to test the things you believe, and we don't like waiting. We've been trained like lab rats for the reward of instant answers. We no longer visit libraries or rifle through microfilm. We don't even read books or wait through long conversations with those older and wiser. We don't turn an idea over in our minds for years. Instead, we have podcasts. We have smooth-talking AIs and search engines and vloggers.

People talk about "doing the research," and by that, they mean they read a few social media accounts, watched a YouTube video, skimmed an article or two in the *New York Times* (or at least saw a screenshot of it). Then they come before others who have been humbly walking in belief for decades, and they suck their teeth and shake their heads and say, Sorry, wrong. Didn't you see the write-up in HuffPost? Didn't you see the documentary on Netflix?

CHURCH

I don't know what softened me. It wasn't one thing. Time, people, experience, the Holy Spirit, all conspired to delicately whittle layers of calloused doom-mongering from my tired heart, and I developed serious doubts about my towering superiority over the hypocrites.

Keeping the whole rage-against-the-hypocrites spirit in red-hot locomotion requires the angry party to think the world of themselves. How had I uncovered the sinister hypocrisy of so many Christians? Because I was so clever! How had I sniffed out their inauthenticity like a truffle pig? I was so much more authentic! After years of assuming these things, traveling the world, spending time with all kinds of different people, thinking the world of myself was getting old. I was even tired of hating myself because that too required an exhausting level of vanity.

When I started talking to God again, when I opened a Bible and started asking questions about who I was and what it was that I was supposed to be doing, one thing became overwhelmingly clear: I wasn't going to figure out the way of Jesus all by myself, and I wasn't going to find the truth purposefully narrowing my range of interaction down to people telling me exactly what I wanted to hear.

My wife and I went back to church. We said to one another, Let's really give this a shot. Neither of us gregarious personalities, we decided that we wouldn't wait for smiling faces to cajole us from a lonely pew, but that we'd insist on our own involvement, that we'd really show up. We signed up to make coffee and vacuum floors. We showed up to a small group. We accepted dinner invitations. No one looked like me or liked the same kinds of things or cared about my impressive life resume of music and travel. I was just some new guy, and I learned to be accepted with gratitude.

People continued to be people. In the years that followed, we hurt people and we were hurt by people. We were sometimes disappointed and angry. We developed meaningful friendships, and some of them ended tragically. We did a lot of apologizing, and we received a lot of apologies.

We learned more about ourselves and experienced more growth, maturity, and formation than ever before.

The New Testament doesn't bother with detailed arguments about the validity of church. It simply presupposes that the only way people follow Jesus is in community with other stumbling, imperfect apprentices. A lot of the New Testament confronts the inevitable complications of those interpersonal relationships and the fallout from sin and failure, and the resounding answer to the chaos of life together is: "Spur one another on toward love and good deeds, not giving up meeting together, as some are in the habit of doing, but encouraging one another" (Heb. 10:24–25).

Now, when I see progressive, sort-of Christians publish think pieces detailing their journey of outgrowing the church, I laugh to myself. When I hear people saying that, for them, a walk in the woods is their church, that dinner with a friend is their church, I think, how convenient, exactly what you're already doing and what you already want to do.

I guess the rest of us need something a bit messier.

It's not that my struggle with self-hate evaporated in an instant or that I suddenly learned to see the beautiful goodness in all people, that we're all inherently "worthy of love." Instead, I was mellowed by the universalism of human inadequacy. Yes, there are false Christians, and yes, there are dangerous and destructive hypocrites who have done severe wounding to the reputation of the church and the people in it. Accepting the brokenness of people is not a permission slip for bad behavior. It is the humility necessary to admit that none of us are always great, none of us have certainty, all of us have doubts, and that if we're going to figure out how to grow, we need each other.

Professor Joseph Hellerman argued that

> spiritual formation occurs primarily in the context of community. People who remain connected with their brothers and sisters in the local church almost invariably grow in self-understanding, and they mature in their ability to relate in healthy ways to God and to their fellow human beings. This is especially the case for those courageous Christians who stick it out through the often messy process of interpersonal discord and conflict resolution. Long-term interpersonal relationships are the crucible of genuine progress in the Christian life. People who stay also grow. People who leave do not grow. . . . It is a simple but profound biblical reality that we both grow and thrive together or we do not grow much at all.[10]

Deconstruction is a convenient escape hatch to avoid the challenges of a life with accountability. The deconstruction movement celebrates a "you do you" herd mentality in which the only evil is the idea of evil itself, which becomes an irresolvable tangle of contradictions. Everyone believes in some kind of objective truth because we can't functionally carry out any other worldview.

The popular deconstructionist quibble is with the suggestion that good things and bad things can be objective—that is, not really up for interpretation. The "you do you" ethos doesn't take kindly to the idea that evil doesn't vary from person to person. In other words, evil is just evil.

The more popular idea is, Hey, depends on you and what you believe! (As long as you adhere to the progressive ideology rule book, otherwise, we will destroy you.) The progressive spirituality social club welcomes deconstructed Christians with open arms as a safe haven from the unforgiving dogma of the church, then imposes on them a new dogma and a new church more ruthless than the first. The veneer of progressivism as a bastion of subjective spirituality crumbles immediately when the once-welcomed deconstructionist uses the wrong political language, supports the wrong artist, tweets the wrong catchphrase. And whereas the teaching of Jesus requires perpetual forgiveness and reconciliation between disciples, the ruthlessness of cancel culture is unforgiving in its permanence.

But if you follow the rules, you can carve out a nice little niche for yourself in the progressive world of deconstructed Christians within the self-affirming echo chamber. You shout the manual into a like-minded mob, and it comes right back, and everyone feels all fired up about the same stuff, and any suspiciously dissenting ideas are torn away with wild barbarism.

But you, reader, you're thinking, Couldn't this be said of this church? You're thinking, Isn't the *church* also a self-affirming echo chamber? A place where ideas and individualism are discouraged and condemned? It can be. But the church has the one idea so unpopular in all the world that it will always escape any accusations of simply telling us what we want to hear.

That idea is self-denial. It is the final Great Predator. Unlike the four predators that preceded it, self-denial is not a corruption of Christian teaching but the fundamental precept on which it is based.

And hardly anyone wants to do it.

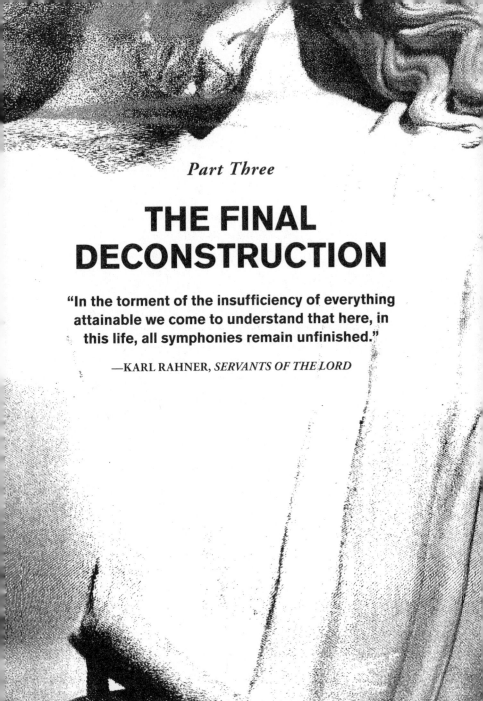

Part Three

THE FINAL DECONSTRUCTION

"In the torment of the insufficiency of everything attainable we come to understand that here, in this life, all symphonies remain unfinished."

—KARL RAHNER, *SERVANTS OF THE LORD*

The Apprentice: Forbidden Fruit

THE APPRENTICE WAS HUNGRY. He was hungry when the light caught the succulent fruit hanging from the drooping branches of trees that lined the narrow road of his discipleship.

He stopped to eat. But when the Apprentice reached for the supple flesh of the ripe fruit, the Master stopped him.

The Master spoke to the Apprentice as a master speaks to a student. "Do not eat the fruit."

A few journeyers passed the Apprentice, heading back the way they came, fruit in hand, the bright red juice of it dribbling down their chins as they ate. The Apprentice's stomach groaned.

"I'm hungry," he told the Master.

"I will feed you," the Master assured the Apprentice. "But do not eat this fruit. The food I give you will do you good. This fruit will hurt you."

The Master invited as he had many times before, "Trust me."

The Apprentice watched as another traveler passed, leaving the road of apprenticeship behind, his arms filled with fruit. A dark, nagging suspicion blossomed within the Apprentice. Why would the Master leave me to my hunger? Didn't he care? Was the Master cruel and power hungry? Was the Master so mean-spirited and insecure that he insisted on testing the Apprentice's faithfulness by starving him?

As the Apprentice considered these things in his heart, he felt the Master's hand on his shoulder. When the Apprentice looked at him, the Master's face was soft with love and compassion.

"Follow me," the Master said.

The Apprentice loved the Master. Though he had heard his teacher's lesson, he began to suspect that maybe this particular lesson was a mistake. Surely, the Apprentice thought, the Master would not have me deny my hunger. Other apprentices who had come before had also written of the fruit's danger, warning against it, but the Apprentice thought it would be nice if they were mistaken. He asked around until he found someone to tell him they were.

He reached for the fruit. When the Master spoke, his voice was steady and clear.

"You cannot eat that fruit and continue walking this road. The way forward is trust. Trust that I will provide what is best. You can take the fruit and head back the way you came, like so many others. But if you so choose, and when the fruit sours in your stomach, you will find me waiting here for you. Ready to lead you again."

The Apprentice understood then what was at stake, and he followed behind the Master, the glimmering fruit mocking his hunger all along the narrow road.

THE LAST GREAT PREDATOR: SELF-DENIAL

"Someone once said there are only two things worth writing about, love and death."

—DONALD RAY POLLOCK

Chapter 11

BROKEN TOOTH, INFECTED SKULL

THE THIRD TIME I shattered one of my incisors, I had no idea how desperately the break would haunt me. It had been a night like any other, screaming and twisting on some sweat-spattered stage in New York, one stop among dozens. It was cause and effect. I hit something. That something hit my microphone. That microphone hit my tooth. My tooth—steadied by my gums—had no choice but to explode.

This is the curse of my crooked teeth. I don't get cavities; I just break them against hard surfaces.

First was the plastic eye of a Kermit the Frog doll lobbed across the room by my older brother, colliding perfectly with soon-to-be ruined enamel. Second, I'd fallen asleep on the floor of our van when a bump in the road introduced my formerly repaired tooth with the iron leg of the bench seat above. Now there was this whole microphone incident.

The order was this: broken tooth, temporary fix, broken crown, incompetent repair, infected skull.

But long before the infected skull, all the way back to the night of shattered incisor number three, a dental assistant witnessed the whole thing and offered to help. He'd been somewhere out in the violent ebb and flow of the humid, stinking mosh pit when it happened.

"I saw the whole thing," he told me after the show. "I think I can help."

By graciously calling in a few favors, this guy had me in a dentist's chair early the next morning before we left for Connecticut. The dentist had agreed to help fit me for a temporary crown, pro bono, but warned that this rushed solution would hold for a few weeks, tops, and that I should plan for a permanent solution as soon as possible.

I did what the dentist told me to do. It just took me sixteen years to do it.

I was about to plant a church. It was, in fact, the very first Sunday of our new church. I didn't feel so great. For the first time in my life, I was facing an undertaking that didn't begin and end with my will to do it. Music, writing, that was up to me. My will. But starting a whole new church? People were depending on me, and I was depending on people. People were expecting things. If the whole thing bombed, I'd be forced to return to my mentors, the ones who had sent me out, empty-handed and defeated. All the stress and anxiety were compounding to the degree that I was physically ill from it. I didn't know that was possible then, so I thought it strange that I'd been struck with a sudden and severe spring cold.

I dragged my aching body to the bathroom of our tiny Portland apartment to clean myself up. My head throbbing, I wound a strand of floss around my index fingers and threaded the space between my front teeth. With a single movement, that temporary crown, the one intended for a few weeks but that had lasted sixteen years, popped free of its time-defying glue, bounced around in the white bowl of my sink, skidding to a stop in a watery, pinkish puddle of blood.

I looked at my puffy, toothless reflection and sighed. Things were not going the way I'd hoped. The ugliness of my toothless visage personified the hobgoblin of my hateful interior world. It was like it was clawing its way up and out of me through my mouth. My wife found me sitting on our bathroom floor with a vacant expression, my crown still in the sink.

God had been asking me to deal with all of this. I wasn't answering on the basis that me not liking myself, in my mind, was sort of like humility. And isn't humility great? But I remembered something Dorothy Day said: "I really only love God as much as the person I love the least."[1] The person I loved the least was me, and I hated me. My hatred of me was not some noble outworking of Christlike humility. I was Narcissus frozen over my reflection in the water. I was frozen by hate.

INFECTION SPREADING

Now, for the first time in my adult life, I had insurance. Now I had dental. In the first dentist chair I'd warmed since those sixteen years prior, a rushed DDS fastened a permanent crown to the broken stump of my original incisor. Later, I'd watch him frown at a dark spot on my X-ray, asking me, "You don't feel any pain right here, do you?" I didn't then, but I would later. He crowned the tooth, and the church plant lumbered forward. This same dentist would eventually be shut down for malpractice, but not before his hasty crown installation set the stage for an infection traveling up the cavernous tunnels of my root canal.

My next dentist would tell me all this, pointing to the now-cloudier spot on a new X-ray. This gray blob between my nose and lips, my new dentist told me, was a bad infection. This is probably why I was toppled by pain one evening cleaning up after a Sunday church gathering. In the months since we'd started the church, both my tooth and my heart had become sick, dangerous places.

For the tooth, I'd need an apicoectomy. My new dentist referred me to a specialist who chiseled my gums away from the bone, drilled into my skull, scraped out the infection, filed down the root, and sewed my gums back together. One assistant was there just to vacuum up all the blood.

Dealing with what was going on in my heart was not as easy. I watched the whole procedure reflecting in the glass lens of the bright light hovering like a sentinel above the violence, and I thought about all the times I'd broken my tooth. It was only after my temporary fix had been left in a pink, pulpy puddle that I was forced to address this thing I'd been avoiding. But the fix wasn't enough.

In the end, the infection had to be scraped out of my head.

STOP WHIPPING YOURSELF

Pieter van Laer was a Dutch artist who mostly painted landscapes and animals. Look him up, and you'll uncover a strange painting of an alley in some European village populated by peasants, beggars, and dogs. Really, what you'll notice is the two bizarre figures dressed like ghosts, whipping their own backs bloody.

These weirdos belong to an all-but-extinct medieval movement called Flagellantism, the members of which notoriously mutilate their own bodies by slinging vicious whips over their shoulders to scourge their backs. Sometime around the fourteenth century, the Catholic Church condemned Flagellantism as a cult, but there are still people around the world who lash themselves in the name of Christianity, Judaism, and Shia Islam.

Why whip yourself? Could be a public statement in response to war, famine, or injustice, like a hunger strike. Could be a means by which one "mortifies the flesh" or, in less antiquated vernacular, a means by which you beat the sin out of your body. I wasn't exactly sure why I was doing it. I didn't bleed my back with a cat-o'-nine-tails, but I was scourging myself as best as I knew how.

When I was much younger, a friend of mine told me that I "get mad and stay mad." They mentioned this in passing, but I never forgot it. At the time, I liked the sound of it, probably for the same reason I choose to maintain a death grip on my anger against people, things, and life. I didn't think of myself as a particularly angry person, but I believed (albeit subconsciously) that refusing to release others from the prison of my unforgiveness made me powerful. I could not control being hurt, betrayed, or disappointed, but concentrating the concussive blast of my animosity on the people and things that did the hurting and betraying and disappointing, this I could control.

It was sad and pathetic, the pettiness of it, and Jesus would not allow me to continue in my apprenticeship unless I gave it up. Eventually,

I started forgiving. Ronald Rolheiser argues that dying with a for-giving heart is the ultimate moral imperative. Our work, Rolheiser reasons, is to forgive those who hurt us, forgive our own sins, forgive the unfairness of our lives, and even forgive God when he turns out to be other than we expected.

I was beginning to learn three out of the four. I won't pretend to have mastered any one mode of forgiveness, but I was learning to practice them. Most of them, anyway. Forgiving myself my own sins—forgiving myself for being me—was, for me, a nonnegotiable. I was resolute in my warm, calcified narcissism, satisfied with the belief that I was doing God a favor by hating myself. I was that ridiculous, laughable rich guy who comes to Jesus, eager for appren-ticeship, but goes away sad when Jesus requires that he part with all of his money and possessions. We read this guy and pity him, the fool. My treasure was my self-obsession, and Jesus was insisting I give it up.

I said to Jesus, You don't understand, I'm doing good things with this.

Jesus said, Put it down.

I said, You don't get it, Jesus. Aren't you the one who told me I had to deny myself? To take up my cross?

Jesus said, This is not your cross. Put it down.

I laughed and tried changing the subject.

Jesus said, You are not listening to me. Put it down.

I said, Look, Jesus, I'd love to help you out, but this is just really im-portant to me, okay? Do you understand that?

He said to put it down.

I said, What if I meet you halfway? What if I do less of it? What if I take it easy on the whole self-obsession and hatred from time to time, huh?

Jesus told me this wasn't enough. All of it had to go.

I was frustrated. Do you know how hard that would be for me, Jesus? For as long as I can remember, this has been me. And hasn't some good come from it? And is it really so bad? And couldn't it be worse?

Put it down and follow me.

Look, Jesus! Look at *them*! Aren't *they* worse? Is what I'm doing really worth all this fire and brimstone? Haven't I put most everything else down? Aren't I at least trying? Will you really deny me over this? Jesus?

But he was walking. I wanted to follow him but found this thing I'd been carrying too heavy for the effort. I could either put it down and follow Jesus, or stop there, and that would be it.

Chapter 12

EVERYONE IS GOING TO HAVE TO DIE

A TWELVE-YEAR-OLD BOY OPENS the heavy steel door of a Philadelphia boxing gym. Inside hang a dozen heavy punching bags, their cracked leather bound in ancient duct tape. Other young men hit the bags with sage-like focus under sweat-beaded brows. An older man approaches this new boy and asks what he's looking for.

A coach, the boy says. I want to learn.

Katherine Dunn, beloved novelist and boxing journalist, wrote about a scene like this one in her book *One Ring Circus*. "A good boxer," she claimed, "is a miracle of chaos and mathematics. When I think about the complex variables required to bring the right kid to the right coach in the right place at the right time, I am amazed that it ever happens at all."[1]

The coach asks this twelve-year-old boy to assume a fighting stance. Then, using only a finger, the coach stabs at the kid's shoulder, and the kid loses his balance.

They go back and forth like this, the kid trying to stabilize his stance and the coach, with a finger, exposing his instability. His point made, the coach points to the sweat-encrusted floorboards, and tells the young man to imagine a square. The coach shows the young man where to set his feet within the imaginary square, and lo, his balance is miraculously set, and, even when poked, the young man does not stumble.

To the world beyond the gym, this scene is an absurd one. But this young man, if he so chooses, will carry this imagined square beyond the doors of that ramshackle gym, out into the world, his school. He'll see that square on his bedroom floor, on his neighborhood sidewalk, and then he will decide if he will bring it back to that gym the next day and the next, and if he so chooses to fan that little flame, it will burn like fire until all of life is the gym and every moment is the training.

The training will require that this boy deny himself the license of those who are not training. He will not eat what they eat, not sleep when they sleep. His days busied with the stuff of apprenticeship, he will willfully deny himself many things he desires, and the denying will hurt. Other young men who entered the gym the same day, who imagined the same square, who experienced the same little flame erupt in their hearts, they will fall away. When they compare the cost of the training to the freedoms and frivolities of nontraining, they will hit their snooze buttons and stop showing up. This, too, will hurt the boy, but he understands. The ask is so high.

No one beyond the gym will ever understand the training, not really. Nor should they. That's okay. Neither this boy nor his coach will walk the streets of Philadelphia barking at vagrants and commuting businessmen, shaming them, demanding they begin their own training. They will not demand nonboxers to crowd their worldly schedules with exercises and drills. They won't prowl the bus handing out meal plans and protein supplements. These other people, they aren't training. What business is it of the coach to train nonboxers?

To the nonboxer, the passerby, the language of the gym would be alien and meaningless, the sacrifices of the protégé without purpose. It was the young man who stepped into the gym and asked for training, not them. The students of that gym belong to a code. Students are not prisoners of their training; it must be chosen, and it must be chosen again and again and again. As long as the training is chosen, the trainees carry their coach's square everywhere they go. They choose what those who are not training would never choose, and they dutifully deny what those who are not training happily indulge.

There will be some in this young man's life who, beholden to his cuts and bruises, inconvenienced by his schedule and diet and the demanding rhythms of his training, will encourage him to hang up the gloves for good. There will be others who are threatened by the young man's dedication. His passion will become a painful spotlight on their own listlessness, and they will chastise his focus as a young life wasted. They will call him less than a person. They will speak to him of the good life, a life he is missing. Or maybe, they will needle holes in his lifestyle, imploring him to soften his commitments.

"Box," they'll tell him, "but not like this."

And maybe these jeering other voices will discourage this young man so that he stops showing up to the gym.

But maybe not.

DO WHAT THOU WILT

Before police learned the name Paul Michael Stephani, he was called "the weepy-voiced killer." Stephani's now infamous 911 calls reveal a man unglued by his crimes, furious and distraught by his inability to curb an arbitrary blood lust.

"Will you find me?" he asked in a call to police in 1981. "I just stabbed somebody with an ice pick. I can't stop myself. I keep killing somebody."

In another call, he sobbed into the phone, "I couldn't help it. I don't know why I had to stab her. I am so upset about it."

He told the police, "I'll try not to kill anyone else."[2]

His attempt at willpower failed.

Stephani, for people like you and me, is a boogeyman, like all serial killers. A mostly unknowable and morbid curiosity that raises one of the oldest questions in the human experience.

If he didn't want to do those awful things, why did he do them?

Why do we do things that we don't want to do? Not really, anyway.

You don't want to make yourself feel sick with another helping of dessert, to stay up late enough to sabotage the following workday, to raise your voice at your kids. You don't want to get drunk, hurt your loved ones, sleep around, buy and see and do things you know won't make you happy.

The porn addict doesn't want to be a porn addict. The drug addict doesn't want to drain their resources, relationships, and health into an overwhelmingly destructive substance. Even criminals and killers often experience a painful internal paradox of being drawn to do things they hate.

One afternoon I was walking into our local supermarket with my son when I noticed a gentleman exiting as we entered. He seemed, at a glance, an average middle-aged suburban dad with his young children. But down the inside of his forearm, I couldn't help but notice his only visible tattoo. In bold black letters that seemed to indicate fresh ink, it read: "Do what thou wilt."

Aleister Crowley at the grocery store.

In 1904, English occultist Aleister Crowley visited Cairo, Egypt, where he claimed to have been visited by a supernatural entity. This being was said to provide Crowley with something he called *The Book of the Law*, which became the basis for a religion called Thelema. For Crowley, Thelema was a mystic spirituality that could perhaps best be described in his famous quote: "Do what thou wilt shall be the whole of the Law."[3]

This line of thinking was carried on and adapted in 1969 by Anton Lavey in *The Satanic Bible*. People think of *The Satanic Bible* as this horrifying ancient tome of dark magic, but really, it's just a collection of essays by a guy with a sinister-looking goatee, published by HarperCollins in the late '60s. For Anton Lavey, *do what thou wilt* elevated the individual to the authoritative seat of God. Consequently, humanity had no need of a higher power, as they would act as their own gods.

It all sounds terribly intense, but you don't need a black cowl and a pitchfork to buy into Lavey's logic. In the early '90s, pop-culture boogeyman Marilyn Manson articulated normalized Satanism when he said: "To me, Satanism was never about worshiping the devil. It's about man being his own god on earth. You do not worship anything except yourself."[4] Well said, Manson.

Jennifer Lopez—of all people—essentially espoused the same view when she said, "My heart is the ruler of all my being."[5] Not counting this guy I passed at the grocery store, you don't hear as much "do what thou wilt" these days. Instead, you hear, "Be true to yourself."

You hear, "Follow your heart."

Oprah, Ryan Gosling, Ellen DeGeneres, Taylor Swift, the Will Smith dynasty, actors, activists, politicians—"Be true to yourself."

But which self are you being true to, exactly? Inside the chaotic storm of all that you are is a collection of desires, many of which conflict with the others. You want to spend more time with your family, or reading, or exercising, or working on that project, but you also want to zone out and tumble headlong into the useless soul-sucking black hole of social media. You want to wake up early, to get more done, but you also want to dedicate hours of your week to bingeing some new miniseries. Which desires are you? If you "do what thou wilt," which thou will do the wilting?

It's not that Jennifer Lopez or Ellen DeGeneres or even Marilyn Manson are formal Satanists, per se, but that they espouse what could easily be argued is satanic philosophy. The presupposition built into "be true to yourself" is that you are fundamentally very good. You are the best option among many in terms of to whom one might be true. Be true to yourself because you are pretty great. If something feels natural, intrinsic, in keeping with your inborn desire, then the most viable option is to honor that thing.

But no one does this. Not really, anyway.

Whatever you think about your brain, how it works, or how it got there, pretty much everyone agrees that it's not entirely trustworthy. Very few people allow themselves complete libertarian freedom to act on their every desire and impulse. Such a thing, almost everyone admits, would be ridiculous and destructive. But why? Who says?

"Love" is a weird, nebulous concept for human beings. Where I live, you can't throw a rock without hitting a "love wins" or "love is love" bumper sticker or yard sign. For some, love is a strong felt sense of affection for someone or something. Love, some would argue, is the freedom to express the desire of your heart without repression. Of course, we have to draw the line somewhere.

Allowing or enabling people to persist in destructive behavior, many would argue, isn't loving. If by "destructive behavior" you mean heroin and murder, few would disagree. But the parameters of "destructive behavior" vary wildly from person to person and can be influenced by anything from upbringing to political allegiances to the kind of accounts one follows on Facebook.

Self-denial isn't so radical a concept after all. Really, everyone believes that someone else should deny themselves, and we all tend to think we know best who it should be, but it sure as heck shouldn't be us. *We* should be free to follow *our* hearts because, after all, we believe the right things, vote the right way, obey the right masters. We're on the right side of history. It's everyone else who should be denying themselves.

Self-denial, in the Jesus movement, is a great equalizer of all who would follow Jesus. Everyone is broken, everyone has gone astray, everyone is going to have to die.

The idea is that, given God's status as Creator of life and the universe, God is likely the authority on how life in the universe works best. The idea is that when human beings live in harmony with God's design for how life works best, things go better for everyone. When humans reject, rebel against, or actively defy God's design, things go poorly for everyone. God is not after blind obedience because he is a capricious rule-monger, but because he is a loving Father.

Again, the parent/child paradigm explains the idea in terms with which few people disagree. A kid wants to survive on an exclusive diet of sugary cereal, pull their sibling's hair, play in the dryer, whatever. A parent knows more about life and the world than the kid does, so the parent lovingly implements discipline and imposes limitations. If the kid acts in accordance with the kid's desire, they'll hurt themselves and other people. Though the kid lacks the broad metaphysical comprehension of why this is true, they can learn to trust their parents through the harrowing life journey of trial and error, obedience, and disobedience. This is the love of the parent, and this is the love of God.

Or, simpler still, God gets mad when his kids touch the stove. Not because he feels strongly about the stove being touched, but because he does not want his children burned. God loves his kids.

But us? We want to touch the stove. We want to touch the heck out of it. And we have our doubts about God's so-called "love." If God loved us, he'd let us touch the stove. Thing is, God *does* love us enough to let us touch the stove. We're free to do it. God is not controlling or coercive. He does not impose his relational love on those who want nothing to do with it. But if you want to know God, if you want to hear what he has to say, he's going to tell you not to touch the stove. It's sort of an "if you live in my house you'll abide by my rules" kind of thing.

Obedience is our inroad to intimacy with the one who created us, who knows and loves us. Albert Schweitzer said, "Follow him and you will know him."[6] Frederick Dale Bruner said, "Obedience to the will of God is the way to the knowledge of God."[7]

SO THAT YOU WILL NOT FALL AWAY

In the fifteenth chapter of John's biography of Jesus, there's a profound agrarian metaphor about knowing God. "I am the vine; you are the branches," Jesus says. "Remain in me, as I also remain in you" (vv. 5, 4, respectively).

Disciples of Jesus live by a code. They obey the teaching and commandments of their Master. But Jesus does not believe the heart of his Master/apprentice dynamic is rule management. Jesus envisions a mystic way of life in which all of the uncomplicated mundanity of minute-by-minute life is anchored in the cosmic union of God's loving presence. That somehow, God's living, active presence is as accessible in the tedium of daily chores as it is in the spiritual euphoria of your most emotionally wrought time of worship.

No one "remains in Jesus" by default. If they did, Jesus wouldn't have bothered pleading with us to do it ten times in one short teaching. This is something we have to practice and learn. The medieval monk Brother Lawrence called it "practicing the presence of God." The more we discipline ourselves with thoughtful, consistent rhythms of bringing our hearts and minds into the presence of God and staying there, the more we begin to feel ourselves stretching comfortably into the spaces between those moments. God is with us in quiet, prayerful meditation on the Scriptures, and he is with us as we wash dishes, a toddler pulling at our pant leg.

If the branches remain in the vine, they bear fruit.

When I talk to married couples, frustrated and discouraged by the ugly distance that has yawned open between them over time, it doesn't surprise me to learn the source of this terminal growth. Communication slowed to a crawl. It got easier avoiding painful topics and conversations than dealing with them. Resentment festered in the void. Time together withered, becoming little more than empty ritual and obligatory rhythm. Love dried up, becoming a brittle husk threatening to crack at the first sign of confrontation.

Deconstruction is like that.

We stop talking *to* God in favor of talking *about* God. We refuse to commit time and energy to our relationship with God and then resent him for not making himself more known in our hour of need. We don't bring our ugly failures and secrets before God or speak candidly with him about the dark things twisting their way up through the lower reaches of our souls. We're superficial and insincere before God, bitter and indignant at the lack of depth between him and us. God becomes depersonalized, a concept, a source of agitated resentment, the spouse who failed us.

No one bothers to ask how we got here or what can be done. It's the other person's fault, and we want out.

Jesus reveals the secret of faithful discipleship—how to survive the Great Predators and the deconstruction—and the answer is as simple as it is profound: "Remain in my love" (John 15:9). Time spent.

Presence. Showing up. Communication. Being there. As in marriage, wage war against any gap that threatens to open between you.

If you do this, Jesus warns, the world will hate you (see John 15:18–25). Immediately after his short sermon on the vine and the branches, Jesus assures his disciples that the world isn't going to approve of their discipleship, but that the Spirit of God—the empowering presence of Jesus, how Jesus is *with* us—will empower them to persevere.

"All this I have told you," Jesus says, "so that you will not fall away" (John 16:1).

Remain in Jesus, the world will hate you for it, but the Spirit of God will empower you for faithfulness. All this I have told you so that you will not fall away.

THIS WAY TO NOWHERE

No one has to follow Jesus. Most people won't. But whoever decides to embark on the narrow, lifelong road of discipleship willingly submits to Jesus's vision for what it means to be fully human, to experience life to the fullest, to reject that which destroys the body and soul. Anyone who wants to follow Jesus has to die.

Our twelve-year-old would-be boxer, the one who strolled through the doors of our theoretical gym a few pages ago, imagine he took his training into his own inventive hands. Imagine his trainer told him, "Hit the bag like this," and the kid, he says, "I don't want to. I want to hit it like this instead." Imagine his trainer tells him, "Eat these things, not those things," but the kid shakes his head and replies, "I don't want to." Imagine the trainer pleads, "Let me wrap your hands before you spar, so you don't break them," and the kid, he snatches his hands back in disgust and says, "I don't want my hands wrapped."

This kid isn't training at all. He could call himself a boxer, I guess, but he isn't one. Whatever he's doing, it isn't boxing.

DISCIPLES OF NOTHING

As long as there has been The Way—those apprenticing with Jesus, embracing and embodying the teaching and lifestyle of Jesus—The

Way has known opposition both inside and out. Jesus himself taught openly that his way of life would not be embraced by everyone, that a lot of the people who sign up would drop out.

I think of Jesus's parable of the sower.

In it, a man plants four sets of seeds. The first set is eaten by birds, the second burns up in the sun, the third is choked out by weeds. The fourth set, against all odds, finally grows. This parable is about the kingdom of God. God's triumphant renewal of all things—the inbreaking kingdom of a new humanity, a broken world restored. How to best capture the power and majesty of this concept in metaphor? Bronze chariots? A stampede of buff warriors? A tidal wave? A hurricane? No. Some farmer planting seeds. Most of which don't grow.

It's not exactly a rousing sales pitch. Jesus's representation of the kingdom of God as tiny seeds—most of which don't grow—was intentional and sobering, and it's as off-putting now as it was then. "And that is why," one scholar notes, "the great majority of the human race will always (if even subtly) reject Jesus."[8]

This, I realize, sounds like a strange presupposition on which to build the movement that will change the world. A minority of success amongst the majority of failure. Authentic discipleship to Jesus, accurately understood, is a small movement with the world against it. This is good or bad, depending on how you look at it. Mark Sayers said it well: "One person's beleaguered minority is another's dedicated, committed core. It's all a matter of perspective."[9]

With a wide enough view, it will always seem as if the world has gone nuts and people are abandoning Jesus in droves. This has been going on since Jesus himself walked around ancient Palestine gathering disciples. Jesus was great at alienating an audience, applying pressure to the hesitations of would-be disciples. Jesus sometimes reads almost like he discourages interested followers. As if when someone accepts his invitation to "follow me," the first thing Jesus asks them is, "Are you sure? Think about it."

When people think about the choice between what they want and what Jesus wants, looking out for number one is the traditional victor. Of course, no one puts it quite like that. We prefer to make heroes of ourselves by describing deconversion as freethinking heroism. Where others are sadly left to their dogmatic bondage, these open-minded trailblazers are now free to pave their own way to god! (Whatever *that* is.)

The deconstruction movement often prides itself on ambiguity, the idea of journeying spiritualists as birds in flight, never settling on a concrete idea, always in motion. But everyone has a theological position on everything. It may not be logical or carefully conceived, but we have them, nonetheless. It sounds oh-so-modern to chase after a worldview that lovingly welcomes the tension of every different mode of thinking and spirituality, but no one lives that way.

We stab little progressive-sounding placards into our green lawns that promise "we welcome all religions, all beliefs," but do we? What about fanatics who bomb abortion clinics? What about White nationalists and those people who sincerely believe Hillary Clinton worships the devil while cannibalizing small children in the secret basement of a pizzeria?

Even claiming to have no position is a position.

We all follow someone or something. Everyone is a disciple. The question is: a disciple of what?

Discipleship to Jesus—like most disciplined, lifelong training—requires that the trainee reject closed-mindedness and intellectual stagnation. The willingness to wrestle with your faith, to build and rebuild, to transform over time, and to learn and practice loving God with all your mind within the slow and patient accountability of life shared in community are all inarguable components of following Jesus.

Christianity has never been afraid of questions and problems and doubt and wrestling because God isn't either. He welcomes it. God is not insecure. God understands that being human is difficult. As a family, Christians agree to wrestle through their discipleship together. To welcome questions and encourage one another. We need disciples full of faith to lend theirs to those in seasons of drought, and we need disciples full of wisdom to speak truth to the lies we are often tempted to believe.

We need disciples who have been walking the road for years, decades, in our midst, to remind us what faithfulness looks like. We need the Spirit of Jesus speaking through our brothers and sisters, words of prophetic encouragement into our lives week in and week out.

All of this requires that we give things up. That we deny ourselves. All of this requires that while the rest of the world hits the snooze button, calls us foolish, oppressed, misguided, we wake up early and head for the gym.

PREPARING FOR YOUR OWN EXECUTION

Elizabeth Bird, a specialist for the New York Library, called Shel Silverstein's *The Giving Tree* "one of the most divisive books in children's literature." She reasoned, "To my mind, you are either a *Giving Tree* fan or you loathe and abhor it."[10]

No one is quite sure exactly what *The Giving Tree* means to communicate with its short, simple story of a tree and a boy she loves. Over the boy's lifetime, the tree gives itself away, apples, branches, trunk and all, for the boy's sake, and the boy mostly just asks for more as the story carries on into his old age.

Is the story about friendship or motherhood? Is it about noble and benevolent self-sacrifice, or is it about abusive codependency? Did the author intend to comment on either thing or simply record fictitious events and leave us to analyze them like a Rorschach test? Good, bad, or neutral—the story is about someone who gives up parts of themselves. This is why, I think, the story was destined for controversy.

Some of the great cliches of fiction are characters caught up in the debate over self-sacrifice. You know the ones: the meek but heroic protagonist who is willing to put themselves at risk for the sake of others. Beside them, the cranky self-preservationist who snorts and invites the hero to wise up, look out for number one. We root for the hero because, under the right circumstances, self-sacrifice is to be celebrated. We know this from life, and we know this from fiction.

But, even in fiction, self-sacrifice sports a tolerance threshold before it tips from admirable to foolish. From noble to ignoble. From loving to unhealthy. Disagreement over the nature of self-sacrifice is at the very heart of our willingness or unwillingness to follow Jesus of Nazareth. In our world of venerated deconversion, the "be true to yourself" mantra is the banner under which innumerable former Christians are marching toward the church exit. Jesus is fine if he doesn't tell us what to do. Or he can tell us what to do, just as long as we like what we hear. As long as it *feels* right.

Both conservative and progressive quasi Christians do this. Everyone is okay with Jesus correcting people they don't like. The Right is happy to have Jesus lecture the Left about gender and sexual identity, but they don't want to hear Jesus talk about porn and divorce. The Left really wants Jesus to give the conservatives a stern talking-to when it comes to social justice and racism, but he better keep his sexual ethics to himself. It just doesn't *feel* right. And yet, denying what often *feels* right, denying ourselves some of the things we want most in life in order to obey Jesus is at the heart of what it means to be a Christian.

We misunderstand self-denial as nauseating fish oil that must be taken to glean some alleged benefits within the unknowable recesses of the body. This not only confuses its purpose, but it puts things too lightly. Jesus did not describe self-denial as a bitter pill but as death. Self-denial is not "trust me, it's good for you" medicine, but a scary and painful dying by which we learn what it means to live.

And Jesus did it first.

As the German theologian Meister Eckhart wrote, "There are plenty to follow our Lord half-way, but not the other half. They will give up possessions, friends, and honors, but it touches them too closely to disown themselves."[11]

Whoever wants to be Jesus's disciple must deny themselves and take up their cross and follow him.

Everyone is going to have to die.

The symbol most commonly associated with the Christian faith is a cross. To many, it means little more than jewelry, a print for leggings, the decorative adornment perched atop an old church building. In the first century, the cross was a symbol of shame and of death. Imagine if the family of one of the Coptic Christians beheaded in ISIS's infamous video selected as the centerpiece for their home a blood-spattered machete.

People would grimace. Turn their heads. Think it in poor taste.

But even that analogy doesn't quite capture the scandal—because a recognized martyr is celebrated as admirable and praiseworthy. So, imagine a mother whose son is executed as a murderer. The painful shame brought on her family. And imagine she then takes to wearing a charm shaped like an electric chair around her neck.

To us, the cross is romantic, pregnant with symbolism and beautifully meaningful resonance. But not to Peter when Jesus first brought it up. Not to the other apostles. To them, the cross was more than defeat; it was the misery, shame, suffering, and humiliation of a criminal condemned to death.

Crucifixion was designed to take a long time. The victim, suspended by rope or nails through the hands and feet, would typically asphyxiate slowly for several agonizing days. Unable to lift themselves enough to draw breath, the victim would succumb to the comprehensive trauma by suffocation, shock, heart attack, thirst, sepsis, or all these things in gradual collaboration.

Contrary to most artistic depictions, victims of crucifixion were stripped naked to further their humiliation. This became a visual display of their powerlessness against Roman might. One first-century philosopher, Seneca the Younger, wrote that victims of crucifixion typically suffered a sharpened stick forced upward through their groin, creating a maddening struggle to suspend oneself against the exhaustion that inevitably lowered the victim down on the spike.

Another ancient Roman writer described crucifixion as "a most cruel and disgusting punishment. . . . The very mention of the cross should be far removed not only from a Roman citizen's body, but from his mind, his eyes, his ears. . . . What shall I say of [crucifixion]? So guilty an action cannot by any possibility be adequately expressed by any name bad enough for it."[12]

The root of our English word "excruciating" is literally "out of crucifying."

This particular method of execution was designed not only to dispose of troublemakers but to inflict maximum physical, emotional, and psychological suffering, and to do so in the public square so that any and all observers would be stricken with horror and fear, thus dissuading would-be criminals and quell would-be rebellions against the Roman Empire.

"Whoever wants to be my disciple must deny themselves and take up their cross and follow me" (Matthew 16:24).

Everyone is going to have to die.

Throughout the centuries, for many disciples of Jesus, this has been a literal death. But for *every* disciple of Jesus, it is a kind of death through self-denial. The least popular in all the modern world of Jesus's teachings. No teaching of Jesus comes with such aggravated offense to the modern sensibility as self-denial. The gospel of our culture is self-fulfillment. The gospel of social media is narcissistic self-celebration. The gospel of entitlement assures us that we deserve comfort, security, entertainment, bells and whistles. If something disrupts said comfort, we have ways of fighting back: more screens, more feeds, outlets for outrage, complaint, pills, apps, porn. "The pursuit of happiness."

The denial of self is a foreign concept. We might deny ourselves in the names of diets and career, to look good and to make money. It is very difficult for us to conceive of a happy, fulfilled life that does not include us getting what we want. We are terrified that if we are denied our dreams, or a soapbox on which to speak, or if we cannot sleep with the person of our choosing, we are less human.

The ever-present antagonism to Jesus's teaching is the modern progressive ideal that it is always wrong—*evil*, even—for anything to stand in the way of another person getting what they want. Any such interference is oppression. If one cannot obtain what they desire, they cannot be happy or realize their full personhood. Nearly everything in the post-Christian cultural milieu screams at us that self-denial is oppression and that self-fulfillment is the only way to authentic happiness and truth.

And yet, here stands Jesus: Everyone must deny themselves, take up their cross, and follow me. Everyone is going to have to die.

AFTER YOU'RE DEAD

When someone accepts the invitation of Jesus to follow behind him in life—him the Master, you the apprentice—something changes. There is an "old" you. This is true regardless of how you feel. When I had my first child, something changed. There was an "old" me who was not a father and a new me who was, whether I "felt" like it or not.

Objectively, I became a father. But the previous years of my life, the time when I wasn't a father, didn't evaporate from the storehouses of my memory. There were old ways of thinking and living that no longer made any sense in my new identity, and occasionally, I defaulted to the old me. If I do this, I don't cease to be a father. It's just that I'm not acting like one.

Each and every disciple of Jesus, just like me, has a lying doppelgänger. Whether they know them or not. It's not an idea I made up. The New Testament calls this liar "the old self." Writers and theologians have called it things like "the shadow side" and "the false self." Brennan Manning called it "the imposter."

Within each and every Christian is another person—a shadowy, misshapen imitation—that masquerades as the real you. But this imposter is insecure. It lives and dies on the approval of people. Maybe the imposter is fretful and obsessive about money and things. It wants to be beautiful but despairs that, really, it is quite ugly. It puts on a show for others, or it cowers in a corner, terrified of people.

The imposter wants to distract the real you with work and achievement, or with sleep, TV shows, and Instagram feeds, with booze and porn, and worse, because the imposter can't sit still. This imposter gossips because it believes tearing other people down will build itself up. It refuses to embrace generosity because the imposter believes it is entitled to what it has.

The imposter is overbusy because it is afraid to slow down, or it is lazy and listless because it is afraid to get up. In Romans, Paul lamented, "I do not understand what I do. For what I want to do I do not do" (7:15). Scholars debate whether Paul is narrating as his redeemed self or in his experience prior to Jesus, but really, either way, he's describing something common to the *human* experience.

A war between two selves. The battle against the false self.

Theologian and monk Thomas Merton said of his false self: "My false self is the one who wants to exist outside the reach of God's will and God's love—outside of reality and outside of life. . . . A life devoted to the cult of this shadow is what is called a life of sin."[13]

All of spiritual formation, Merton argued, is a series of deaths to the false self.

If you follow Jesus, this old version of you served a different master: your old desires. You were at the mercy of whatever you wanted, for better or for worse. To say yes to Jesus is to say no to innumerable competing options. No to shopping however I want, spending my money however I want, eating however I want. No to hyperindividualism, no to social media image curation, no to me-first, careerism, getting ahead, being liked, the American dream. No to my sexuality expressed however I want.

Instead, the disciple of Jesus, by definition, says to his or her Master: What you say to do, I will do. Where you say to go, I will go. You are the Master; I am the apprentice.

Of course, it's easy to pick on our culture's apprehensiveness to the invitation of Jesus, but it was a tough sell back in the first century as well. Jesus knew that the invitation to take up a cross would be widely rejected then and now. Of this inevitability, Jesus said: "Whoever wants to save their life will lose it, but whoever loses their life for me will find it" (Matthew 16:25). Trademark Jesus candidness. These are the options. The only two options.

If "do what makes you happy" is one's highest aspiration, what is there to do but chase the carrot dangling from the stick? Every time we get close enough to take the bite we believe will satisfy us, the carrot replenishes, and, with it, our hunger. What if the chase destroys you and others around you? We can all see this as a metaphor for substance abuse, but we're less prepared to apply the same image to socially acceptable addictions like smartphones and social media, your career, your diet and fitness, a relationship, your marriage, your children, whatever.

When satisfaction with life is contingent on you getting what you want, and when the things you want can all be taken from you, you live out your fragile days walking on eggshells. Because desire is often unfulfilled—it is a bottomless pit, an abyss, much like the soul of the one who chases it. This is the life of following the self. Dissatisfied, disintegrated, ruled by desire, enslaved by want.

This is one of the two options.

The other is this: deny the self, follow Jesus.

It's not, as the Buddha assumed, that desire is always and inherently bad. It's that we're bad at ordering our desires in such a way that they cultivate a lifestyle of self-sacrificial love. But imagine a life of desire rightly ordered according to the way of Jesus. There'd be no concern for impressing others, for status or accumulation. There'd be no anxiety about money, no tyranny of want, no slavery to lust or greed or gossip or laziness.

With desire rightly ordered, we learn to see everything good as a gift. Gratitude becomes a way of life. We learn to see other people, friend or foe, as objects of God's affection, and we learn to treat them accordingly.

Imagine a person who, like all of us, wanders in and out of the storms of life. They rejoice like anyone would, and they suffer like everyone does—but the true source of their joy and steadiness, their reason for being, is unshakable.

This is the life of a person who has given their life away. Lose your life and save it, or save your life and lose it. Jesus taught these as the only two options.

This is the invitation of Jesus. And it begins with a cross. Dietrich Bonhoeffer famously paraphrased Jesus in his book *The Cost of Discipleship*, "When Christ calls a man, he bids him come and die."[14] All of discipleship is predicated on our ability or inability to realize this prerequisite.

Dallas Willard described self-denial as

> the overall, settled condition of life in the kingdom of God, better described as "death to self." In this and this alone lies the key to the soul's restoration. Christian spiritual formation rests on this indispensable foundation of death to self and cannot proceed except insofar as that foundation is being firmly laid and sustained.[15]

What Jesus called "life to the fullest" can never be realized except through the narrowing crucible of self-denial. Everyone is going to have to die.

THE HURT BUSINESS

A popular strategy for silencing one's political or social media opponents is to leverage pain and injustice as the primary qualifications for who is allowed to comment on what. In this system, "easy for you to say" becomes the immediate and final discrediting of anyone deemed unworthy of speaking. Whoever suffers the most is the most qualified and worthy to speak. Lives of comfort and privilege nullify the opinions of the unworthy.

I believe in the existence of privilege and the necessary nuance of empathy and listening, but I take comfort in knowing that within Christianity, all of us have a lot of dying to do. The way of Jesus becomes a shared experience of painful growth and maturity for every apprentice who accepts the invitation to lift their heavy cross. That twelve-year-old Philadelphian boy will receive the same training as every other boxer his coach has trained, but different aspects of that training will be uniquely challenging for each pupil. This is the hurt business.

There will be seasons of life in which it seems you are paying more than someone else. When it seems as if your cross is heavier. A mentor of mine sometimes says, "Pain is pain." He says that people tend to assign unique values to various types of trauma and that while there are different types of trauma with different effects on different people, trauma is trauma.

For one person, giving up the pursuit of money, security, and comfort might seem even more far-fetched than giving up a relationship or a sexual identity. For another, the call of simplicity and generosity is fine, but if the ask is celibacy, the ask is too much. We all have desires, things that we believe we need to make us happy. To follow Jesus, all of them are going to have to take a seat beneath the Master. They will be rearranged, edited, and transformed, but many of them will simply have to die.

It often seems as if there's a digital ticker-tape parade for the courageous individual who denounces faith. They write books, start podcasts, publish blogs. They make a lot of money. But bailing out is easy. Anyone can do that. Many people do. They've been doing it for hundreds of years. Of course, it isn't framed as such. The lament of the deconstructing is one of helplessness. I tried so hard, but I simply could not carry the heavy weight of faith.

Carrying the weight is not easy, but it is being carried. All over the world, amongst all kinds of people for hundreds of years, it is being carried in the shared strength of communal love.

Faithfulness is difficult. And faithfulness is costly. This is why, in all four Gospels, we read the central prerequisite for discipleship to Jesus is: Deny yourself. Take up your cross. In fact, Luke even adds an extra word in his account: Not just "take up your cross and follow me," but "take up your cross *daily*" (see 9:23).

You cannot control desire outright. You cannot select and implement emotions at will. No human can. But you can influence desire. You can influence your emotions. You can reshape the will, slowly, over time. You do this with your habits, lifestyle rhythms, day-to-day decisions about time management, words, purchases, meals, relationships, and on down the list.

Disciples of Jesus train and practice in the way of their Master so that they are becoming, more and more over time, the kinds of people who can say no to destructive desires and yes to the ones in keeping with the heart of God. All healthy parents, on their best days, are willing to afford their children short-term pain and discomfort (to discipline them) to love them well, to teach them what is best, to keep them from harm. The pain and discomfort of self-denial become the ways we learn what it means to walk in the joyful freedom of wanting what God wants.

Augustine believed that humans are made in God's image but that when we allow our desires to become disordered, we suffer as a result. Freud argued that human beings are animals compelled by instinct for pleasure and that when we repress our desires, we suffer as a result.

Not doing what you want to do? Well, that's inauthentic! There are no hashtags for such a thing.

The disciple of Jesus embarks on the lifelong work of crucifying the old self—not entertaining or placating or coddling every desire. Instead, we cultivate, nurture, and develop the things of the Spirit. The things of the flesh we nail to a stake and leave for dead. Again and again and again and again. And on that same stake hangs the mantras of the flesh: Be true to yourself, #dowhatmakesyouhappy, follow your heart.

Left to rot with the old self.

Again and again, day after day. Jesus was crucified to show us how. Now we follow in his example. This is a way of life.

We are so like small children before God, our Father. You don't have to be a parent to recognize this familiar picture: A child unwilling to try that new bite of food, to open their eyes before an image they worry will frighten them, to put a foot in the water, to hold a frog, to board the roller coaster. And the parent beside them, assuring, pleading, Trust me! The parent who knows the child better than they know themselves.

And like children, you and I fret, kneading our knuckles, unable to imagine that God might be after our joy. He wants us to be well-behaved, stoic, spiritual, benevolent, sure. But joy? We're less convinced.

Ignatius of Loyola once defined sin as the "unwillingness to trust that what God wants is our deepest happiness."[16] I no longer feel fit to carry the weight of my own satisfaction. I do not want to attempt to satiate that profound longing with things that spoil and that spoil me. This wrestling inside me, the warfare in here and out there, all of it hangs on this: our ability to look into the eyes of God the Father with trust, and taking his hand, allow him to lead us.

Even though he will lead us to a cross.

Chapter 13

THE SERMON IN THE SUICIDE

MOST OF US, WE didn't plan on ending up where we did. Something feels missing. We wanted to climb a holy mountain and find God there. We romanticized boxing movies and kung fu masters. We wanted to be the young journey-wearied apprentice dragging themselves, blistered and bruised, across the threshold of the master's domain. Once inside, we'd beg him to train us. We'd give up everything for it. We wanted to be Luke in the swamps of Dagobah, Rocky Balboa pummeling a side of beef. We wanted to leave behind the mediocrity of the status quo, peer behind the boring veil of smallness that surrounded us on all sides, and seize all that *more* promised us by years of inspirational after-school specials.

And then we didn't.

We were going to be different from our parents who had buried their heads in the sands of the American dream, who married young, had kids, then retreated to suburbs and jobs they hated until they retired to cable TV and the encroaching dread of all things technological. We grew up slower, defied convention, got married later, changed jobs like pants.

And something was missing.

We found ourselves standing before the priests and popes of self-help and digital fame. We opened our mouths and waited for influencers to place the Eucharist of likes and follows on our eager, drying tongues. We knew we were special. Everyone said so. Though it resisted, the world was going to open for us like a stubborn oyster, and we were going to devour the salty meat of all that was coming to us.

We wanted to leave home. Most of us did. Our moms made us tuck in our shirts every Sunday morning. Our dads made us say our prayers before meals. For our aunts and uncles, the most important thing about Jesus was that he was a Republican. Our grandparents used Leviticus as a weapon against our tattoos. So we wanted to leave home. We wanted our shirts thoroughly untucked, our meals thoroughly unblessed. We wanted to denounce the political god of our aunt's Facebook page. We wanted to say the f-word.

Our parents and their parents, theirs was a religion of obligation—a social contract. God-fearing Christians were respectable citizens, moral guardians. God-fearing Christians were responsible adults, but we were not interested in responsibility nor adulthood. We sang songs about it.

We were going to move to New York, to California. We were going to get a studio apartment and eat Chinese food and lead wild, meaningful lives. Untethered. Unchained.

And maybe we did. But something was missing.

Something inside of us—some desperate stubborn thing—was always reaching out to take hold of what it could never seem to grasp. We tried feeding it experiences and projects. We tried feeding it admiration and accolades but it would not eat them. It would reach out, pull back nothing, and whimper pathetically somewhere in the distant thrum of our hearts. We didn't like the sound, but a wave was coming to drown it out.

We didn't like what we heard, so we buried it under the drip-feed of digital information overload. We trained in the ways of the TV miniseries and online porn. We posed for pictures. We knew that the pictures weren't real and that everyone else knew that the pictures weren't real, but everyone pretended, and that made us feel a little better, at least for a little while, and that was something.

Our eyes glazed over. We forgot about Saturday morning cartoons, waiting through commercials. We forgot about years of algebra tests. We forgot about "please allow six to eight weeks for delivery." Everything started showing up instantly. If it didn't, we complained. Anything that required time wasn't worth it. Expertise no longer mattered. We so dulled our once hungry attention spans that we no longer had the attentive wherewithal to endure a single meal or movie or conversation or get-together without our itchy twitching trigger fingers stabbing at a touch screen.

The God of our parents' Bible was too solid, too concrete. We needed a God open to interpretation. A formless lump of cosmic Play-Doh. We took God by the nape of his neck, and we dragged him, kicking and screaming, into our brave new world. We shook God by the shoulders until his ancient commands and pronouns fell from him like wrinkled apples, and he/she/it became nebulous, a cloud formation for us to squint into while saying smart-sounding things. God became for us something everyone could see their own way.

I see an energy. I see an all-mother. I see a giraffe.

Somewhere in the cavity of our souls, something kept reaching and weeping, and it would not feed on our new cloud god.

We were waiting for the promise of our grade-school bookmarks to come true: you can be anything. Mostly, we wanted to be happy. If anyone asked, we'd say we were. Happier than ever, actually. The happiest we've ever been. Sometimes we believed it when we said it, but that hungry thing inside threatened to expose us as liars, so we kept pushing it down until it became a distant cry, like someone almost dead, its voice a sad decrescendo beneath the pillow we used to smother it.

The fire inside went on burning, and we didn't know whether to fan the flames or douse them with the cold water of reality. We were looking for something, someone to whom we could give our lives, a movement or cause or fad diet. Something. Something big. Something meaningful. We wouldn't be Daniel LaRusso doing chores for Mr. Miyagi, wax on, wax off. No, we'd be Bruce Wayne dragging our collapsing bodies over the threshold of the League of Shadows, desperate for training. Desperate for revelation. We'd be the Bride apprenticing Pei Mei in the Chinese wilderness learning his Five Point Palm Exploding Heart Technique.

Sure, it'd be tough, but we'd find something, and we'd give everything to it. When we convulsed in agony, the chemical burn eating its way through the thin flesh of our hand, Tyler Durden would show us the puckering scars of his own wound and we'd know he'd been there before us and we'd endure.

When we couldn't find Mr. Miyagi, when Yoda and Batman and Tyler Durden turned out to be pipe dreams, we thought about gods or no gods. We went looking for masters, for politicians and pastors. We went looking for gurus. We went shopping for housewares and we bought the best sellers on the best seller endcaps of our department stores. We went looking for the secret. We were going to be a self-made man. A girlboss. We bowed before digital gods and the useless cryptocurrency of online brand management. We gave up carbs.

We were going to know more and be more than the culture that reared us. We chose new masters, new things to believe. Sometimes we chose them to hurt someone else—our parents, our teachers, the small town we left behind. We wanted a new movement. What was most important to us was that this new movement look entirely unlike the one we had been handed at birth.

The old movement was a sheep pen. A herd. It was a rule-based hierarchy based on saying and doing the right things in order to maintain good standing, to belong. The old movement was an antiquated moralism of someone else's design suspended on the brittle wire of ancient answers to modern questions. The old movement wanted us to wipe our feet on the mat, to remove our hats indoors, to say the Pledge of Allegiance. The old movement came with a uniform.

The new movement welcomed us in. All of us had been spit from the unforgiving maw of the same old world. Everyone there was eager to take the old movement apart, to deconstruct it, to move on. Onward and upward. Everywhere we looked, someone was telling us we were right. We fed our sadness a steady diet of frustrated cynicism, and our cloud god became increasingly shapeless, indistinct to the point of nonexistence. But what did it matter? This was all part of the deconstruction, the moving on.

Onward and upward.

We learned a new language. We didn't realize it at first, but there were new rules. There were things you did and didn't say. There were good guys and bad guys. We didn't realize it until we'd been wearing them for a long time, but we'd traded in our old uniforms for new ones. The new uniform hardly looked different at all, but that was okay. We chose to believe it was.

We knew more now. We were smarter. We'd outgrown the old things. We'd evolved. Deconstructing was evolution. Only sometimes, we felt as if we'd not so much evolved as changed sides. We were doing the same thing on the other team. Sometimes we felt as if we'd traded one herd for another, one dogma for another, one rule book for another. We were promised ambiguity, but things turned out to be a little more settled than we'd hoped. There were black and whites, there was objective truth dressed up like mystery, and we wanted so badly to believe it that we somehow convinced ourselves it was so. It wasn't.

Sometimes it felt good, being smarter and better, being on the right side of history. We constantly reminded ourselves of the inarguable awfulness of that sad Christian world we'd left behind. We sat around talking about it, patting each other on the back for our brave escape from it all. We let the world know, and the world loved us for it. Maybe our parents worried, or our grandmas complained, but this made martyrs of us and we loved it. We refused to receive anything other than praise, and anything that contradicted our new herd we translated as persecution, and we loved that too. It made us powerful.

We knew we were right because we *felt so right*. We felt sorry for the sad, deluded souls the world over who had walled themselves up in a dogmatic, unthinking ivory tower of assumed spiritual superiority because that's not at all what we were doing.

Not at all.

THE WAY OUT IS ORTHODOXY

I used up most of the teenage angst and the existential dread of my early adulthood on the burdens and woes of the deconstructionist. I'd been dealt a bad hand: a heart lit with the fires of rebellion in a world desperate to hammer me into the same obedient shape as everyone else. The church world of my formative years was unthinking, cruel, violent, hateful, addled by lazy, racist nationalism. The only thing more dangerous than not stepping out of line was inferring in any way that the line should not exist.

Christians followed rules. We followed the rules we liked and explained away the other ones (the ones that were hard for us or that called our comfortable way of life into question). God didn't have much to say about our wealth and wars, our idols and disobedience, but he was absolutely incensed over gay sitcom characters and R-rated movies. Our job was to white-knuckle America's moral collapse in our nice, neat little homes and nice, neat little churches until God took us all to heaven in the rapture and the whole rotten world went up in nice, neat little flames.

I tried to find myself in it and couldn't. If this was Christianity, if this was the church, I wanted out. I wandered out of one mob and into the other.

The other side of the aisle looked almost exactly like the one I'd left, just with a different outfit. It was still football, just another team. We were aimless and hypocritical, telling ourselves only what we wanted to hear. We dismembered Jesus, Buddha, Nietzsche, and New Age only to sew them back together with all the graceful expertise of fast food and reality television. On whose authority? Ours! We asked very little of ourselves and sat around patting each other and ourselves on the back for not being like those *other* poor, hoodwinked fools.

The way out, for me, was neither the hardened distortion of the Christian movement known as American evangelicalism nor the amorphous "you do you" spirituality of the deconstructionists. The way out was orthodoxy: right belief.

Orthodoxy is the communal foundation of the early, subversive grassroots movement once known as The Way. Orthodoxy is the resolve of more than two millennia of rebels—intellectuals, theologians, philosophers, artists, doctors, pastors, and ordinary men and women—who have refused to succumb to the ebb and flow of the domesticated civil religion or to deconversion, the path of least resistance.

Orthodoxy is the steadfast commitment to the inspiration and authority of the Scriptures, to the lifelong effort of becoming a people of the book, the hard work of study and meditation to unpack the inexhaustible riches within, to unpack its mysteries together, to allow it to shape us and never the other way around.

Orthodoxy is the unwillingness to abandon the church. It is the gracious humility necessary to drag the bruised, limping heap of imperfection that we are into the messiness of shared life and to hold one another up, hold one another accountable, hold one another to the truth.

Orthodoxy is Christianity, the life born of death, the student who walks behind the Master, feet blistered on the narrow road of discipleship.

Orthodoxy is an enormous countryside. Everyone who lives there must do their best to arrange the things of orthodoxy into practices and lifestyle, and not everyone agrees on exactly how this is done best. Thus, within the borders of that great countryside are camps. The camps can be good or bad, depending. When the camps are good, they house humble, gracious Christians who understand that all the camps along the countryside are doing their best. That no camp is perfect. They move freely between the camps to learn from one another, to love and serve one another.

When the camps are bad, they become angry fallout shelters wreathed in barbed wire and encircled with Keep Out warnings. They hide out, spending a lot of time worrying about and villainizing the other camps and the people in them.

Some of these camps are so walled off from the others that they beat down and break those within so that rather than leaving the camp they leave orthodoxy altogether, not realizing there were other places to make their theological homes. Some others, regardless of camps, pack their bags and say, I no longer believe Jesus was raised. They say, I don't want to live here anymore. And we plead with them to stay, but they cannot be convinced, and they leave. We send others out to bring them back.

Sometimes they do and sometimes they do not.

CHOOSE A STORY

I can't tell you your story, but I can tell you mine. Joan Didion famously wrote, "We tell ourselves stories in order to live."[1] Really, everyone believes a story. It's how we understand the world.

"We look for the sermon in the suicide," she wrote.

All human beings experience a nagging pull toward belonging. A scattered few of us (read: the author) experience a concurrent but opposing pull toward alienation. I want to belong, but I want to be an island unto myself. I want deep connection and profound intimacy, but I want to be so unlike anything or anyone that I defy all sense of convention. For much of my life, I struggled against what I believed to be the confining normalcy of the ancient tradition to which I belong. I was standing inside a story that stretched out behind me for centuries and into the distance ahead with no end in sight, and I was pulling at my shirt. I was tapping my foot.

This is a story I tell myself in order to live: You are different. You are special.

I believe stories about dinosaurs and asteroids. I believe stories about the truth in the lie. The food in the commercial is fake. There's a man inside the rubber Godzilla suit. The money-back guarantee is a bluff. We believe stories, for better or for worse, and we believe that we are above the con, that we can see the strings. We tell ourselves stories that wall us off from other stories to protect ourselves from the things we're afraid to believe. We pretend to believe in the goodness and validity of many stories—of every story—the stories themselves becoming vicious ravens pecking at one another in violent panic. We claim that we do not believe in any story, and this too is a story, a snake with its jaws fastened around its own tail, jaw unhinged from the work of it.

The only way we can make sense of the relentless mystery of everything is through the organizing structure of story. No one is born with incontrovertible metaphysical certainty of any meaning or purpose inherent in existence or in the universe. We inherit stories, and we make certain decisions about how far we are willing to carry them as we all go about our march to the grave. Some of us are given stories about Jesus. Others are handed Zeus or Allah or Vishnu or Nietzsche. Everything matters. Nothing matters. Maybe life crawled into the universe on the microscopic surface of clay crystals, or maybe all of this is a flicker on the color display of a simulation.

Everyone believes something. Everyone believes a story.

Maybe you don't want to follow Jesus. Lots of people don't.

In my years as an apprentice and a pastor, I have sat with innumerable men and women, young and old, desperate for the loophole, for the secret that deep down, they knew did not exist, and if it did, the other side of that loophole wouldn't be so great, not really. They want to have their cake and eat it too. They want what was promised by smooth-talking commercials and electric fat-burning belts. Eat whatever you want and still lose weight! Get your degree by mail without any tests! Inherit the kingdom without the king!

They plead with me, eyes full of want, desperate to somehow follow Jesus without having to die. They want to train, they want apprenticeship, but without taking up their cross. They want Jesus, but they don't want Jesus to strip from them a bank account, a career plan, a relationship, a title, a dream, a smartphone. They want Jesus, but not if he makes them poor, bored, celibate; not if he wants them to go to church and fraternize with broken people; not if he pries the protective armor from our soft, supple hide.

Furious that Jesus would have the audacity to ask such a thing—furious and disbelieving—they retreat beneath the protective umbrellas of denial. Maybe Jesus *wouldn't* ask me to do these things I don't want to do. Jesus wants me happy the way *I* want to be happy. They look upon the gnarled, unforgiving wood of the cross meant to kill them, and they say, "No, thank you." Instead, they fashion their own crosses from weightless foam, decorated with slogans and bumper stickers, festooned with plastic jewels and fashion accessories. Isn't this nice, they say. Isn't this easier? And I propose: Maybe you don't want to follow Jesus. Many people do not. *Most* people don't. It sounds like you could be one of them.

It's up to you. You won't have all the answers, only decisions that you choose to make again and again in the chaotic madness of life and ambiguity. All of us choose masters. You can know God, but you cannot exhaust your knowledge of God. His supreme otherness will defy the restrictive fences you erect to control him, to box him in. God will be monolithic in his cosmic otherworldliness, but he will be paradoxical and knowable and intimate. He will be Father and friend in his still small voice. Your role will be loving obedience. Your role will be surrender to the gravity of love. Or not. All of us choose masters. You may choose the Master revealed in the ancient tradition laid out and handed down by millions of people over centuries of life around the world in sacred texts and teaching, or you may choose to flee the loving accountability of family and to deconstruct God, remold and repurpose God so that he fits in your pocket. Redecorate God with your own ideas and ideologies, give God a makeover, start a new club. This new god will be your master.

It's not a question of masters or no masters. It's a question of Jesus or every other master. All of us choose masters.

Choose this day whom you will serve.

(Before We End)

IN THE SPRING OF 2018, I decided to kill myself. To write about it now and imagine that it will be read, I mostly feel ridiculous. This is not an author's trick to win your trust or to demonstrate my sincerity. It's just an ugly story of the way one man indulged his misery and thought about quitting. To put this man on these pages now, I hardly recognize him, but he existed, and I remember him. Remembering him is important.

Years later, a winter storm covered my city in snow. For three days, my wife and I walked with our three kids (one of them in her womb, then) to a nearby hill to sled. Everyone was laughing, our cheeks cherried by the cold, beaded ice in the wisps of my daughter's hair that fell in shimmering tangles from beneath her knit hat. God was with us.

In the early morning hours, I sat by my living room window with my Bible, the snow a phosphorescent lamp as the predawn haze of pink clouds crawled across the horizon, and the temperature inched upward, and the icicles lining the rain gutters danced their rhythmic drip, and my heart was flooded with a dull ache, the quiet beauty of everything.

Nothing was perfect. The ordinary stresses and failures of life gathered about the perimeter of everything lovely. I was telling God that I was sorry for some screw-up. I was worried about a couple of things.

Catholic priest and theologian Ronald Rolheiser wrote about prayer, likening it to the rhythmic and dutiful daily visits that one might pay to their aging parent in a care facility.[1] Every morning, this son or this daughter makes the same drive to the same place and does the same kinds of things. Maybe this person has siblings, and maybe those siblings don't visit as often or at all.

Morning in and morning out, when this son or daughter visits their parent, the visits are often (if not typically) unremarkable. This person sits with their parent. They talk, change sheets, tidy up, share breakfast. From time to time, a visit births a kind of conversation imbued with profound emotional catharsis. From time to time, something happens in these ordinary exchanges that deepens the intimacy and connection between parent and child, and this person leaves with new, life-changing knowledge about themselves and the world around them. But often, they simply sit together and talk and carry out their simple and unglamorous routine.

Sometimes, this person would rather be somewhere else.

Maybe a time comes when this person who has spent years visiting their aging parent this way has a conversation with one of their siblings who doesn't visit much or at all. During this exchange, this person realizes something incredible. The sum total of these years of ordinary and mostly unremarkable visits is this: they know their parent.

This sibling who didn't visit doesn't seem to know their parent at all.

I'm a hopeless romantic. A deeply relational and wildly emotional person. I tend to romanticize what it means to really know someone until it becomes an indie drama film or a Greek tragedy. Really knowing someone, I once believed, meant walking with them through hell and back, unpacking the depths of the soul and arranging its contents naked and lurid in plain view of another, writing songs about it. I have loved my wife for many years, and our relationship has stretched out long enough to house all these things, the trials and brutal honesty and love letters and poems. But really, anyone could have done that. It doesn't take much, and it doesn't take long.

What makes the connection I share with my wife unique in all the world now and forever is time and faithfulness. My wife and I were together before my kids were born, and we will be together when they leave our home. We go to sleep next to each other and we wake up the same way. Our lives together have and will be punctuated by incredible moments of adventure and emotional ecstasy, moments of pain and harrowing uphill reconciliation, but most days, we sit together. Most days, we talk, change sheets, tidy up, share breakfast.

MAYBE I WON'T QUIT AFTER ALL

As the spring of 2018 threatened to become summer, I went back and forth on the whole suicide thing. I'd rewritten and reread my list of pros and cons to the point of memorization. I didn't want to be one of those hasty suicides. I needed to figure this out.

Mostly, though, my mind was made up: June 12, 2018.

I'd survived the deconstruction of my younger years with my faith intact, but it turned out that faithfulness had not erased my brokenness or my pain. I talked about God, I taught the Bible, and I believed everything that I said deep down to the very core of my being. Even so, another part of me was breaking down, and I was preparing for a second deconstruction greater and more final than the first.

And as I barreled forward on the unstoppable bullet train of time toward what I was almost entirely convinced would be my last birthday alive, I kept smiling and laughing. I still shook hands and gave hugs and ordered takeout. I still held my son every afternoon when I arrived home from work, and he rushed toward the car, giddy with excitement. I was preparing to denounce Jesus once and for all. I was preparing to execute the ultimate and most conclusive deconstruction of all.

I was still reading my Bible, still praying. I was talking to God through all of this. Talking but not listening. Until God shouted at me.

The picture came to me one morning as I stood peering from my living room window. Everyone else in my house was asleep. It was very quiet. A cold, coiled darkness had settled in my heart, and I was thinking about dying. I was wallowing in my unhappiness. My self-loathing had been, for most of my life, a lanky black imp that, from time to time, crawled up from my back to perch on my shoulder and whisper cruel nothings in my ear. Not an audible detached voice, but an inner heckler that had become remorselessly abusive. It called me a name, this thing, and I believed it.

The violence of my self-loathing had become so unbearable that it devoured everything good. All of life I saw peering through the jaws of a hungry monster that was eating me, and I believed, *really* believed, that everyone and everything in the whole world would be better if I wasn't in it. Imagine the narcissism it takes to assume this kind of significance.

I'd been thinking a lot about the world without me in it, and the thought comforted me. I knew that people would grieve, that people would hurt, that they'd be angry and upset, but I'd also seen the way the world carries on after it hurts, and I was sure that after the brief season of hurt, my wife, my kids, my friends, my family, my church would all breathe a subconscious sigh of relief. My leaving was like chemotherapy. It would hurt, and it would be hard, but then things could get better.

Of course, none of these things were true. After years of therapy and being mentored, after years of community, prayer, and spiritual formation, I can see these lies for what they were. In the time before and the time after, Thomas Merton was hitting the same nail on the same head. "Despair is the absolute extreme of self-love. It is reached when a person deliberately turns his back on all help from anyone else in order to taste the rotten luxury of knowing himself to be lost."[2]

Abandoning the "rotten luxury" of corrupted self-love is easier said than done. Usually, it requires an intervention of some kind followed by years of hard work and accountability rewiring your heart and mind. Me? I figured I would need some real *A Christmas Carol* level stuff. I was the Ebenezer Scrooge of despair, and I would need three spirits and then some. I needed every person who ever loved me encircling me, pleading with me, holding up pictures of all my happiest memories. Instead, there were no visions of a future worse for my absence, no Christmas spirits, no interventionist, and no weepy slideshow.

What God said about the whole thing came to me one morning as I stood peering from my living room window. In a moment, with my mind elsewhere, God implanted an image in my mind's eye of such forceful, vivid clarity that what I saw changed everything.

I saw my son at the window waiting for his dad to arrive home from work and not understanding that he would never come.

Inside, the coiling thing that had been strangling my heart loosened, and I said, "Okay, God."

I said, "What do I do now?"

It was the death of my deconstruction.

The Apprentice: Death to Deconstruction

THE NARROW ROAD HAD become an uphill battle that few of the Master's followers cared to sustain. The Apprentice watched them as they went, downhill, the path of least resistance, dozens of them at a time. The wind against him, his legs shaking, the Apprentice squinted through the rain, the snaking white filaments of lightning that bisected the dark dome of sky overhead. He was trying to see the Master.

It seemed as if everyone who had walked with the Apprentice was gone. He felt lonely and afraid. He listened to the grumbling of those who passed on their way back down, heading back the way they'd come. Their pain and frustration sounded like his, and he imagined joining them. It felt as if everything—the wind, the others, even the current of his own heart—was pulling him away from the Master. He felt the strength in his legs waiver. He stumbled.

The Apprentice peered behind him and watched as those who had renounced the journey found one another below. They linked arms in their retreat, their faces masks of joy and relief. They were coming together around the cause of turning back, around falling away, and the wind was no longer against them. All of them looked very similar, as they had come from similar places at similar times, and this too comforted the Apprentice because they looked like him. The Apprentice began to pivot, if only slightly.

And then the Master called his name.

The Master's voice was not harsh. Not even corrective. It was gentle but self-assured, punctuated by a probing question mark. The Apprentice knew then the significance of the moment, what was at stake. He watched the former apprentices gathered below in what looked like happy comradery. He considered for a moment all he was prepared to leave behind. Before beginning his descent, the Apprentice drew a deep breath and turned to see the Master.

The Master's face was calm, though the world around him was torn by hardship and trouble. While the former apprentices were finding relief on the way down, the uphill climb looked more unforgiving than ever. The trees that lined the narrow road were bent by the gale, the Master himself drenched by the storm. But then a flicker of movement somewhere in the distance caught the Apprentice's eye.

As the winding journey upward carried on into the distance, the Apprentice could see that there were others still climbing. There were hundreds of them, thousands, millions, and more. They were battered, bruised, and bedraggled by the journey, but on they went. There were too many to count, too many to compare, but the Apprentice could see they were all ages and colors, all ethnicities and nationalities, that they'd come from all over the world to walk the road, men and women and children, and on they went, following the Master, against the storm.

And it occurred to the Apprentice that he would rather be forgotten than remembered for giving in.

Below was the deconstruction. The siren call to take all of it down, to leave all of it behind. Above was the transformation: the slow and painful lifelong work through questions and doubts, learning and growing, being wrong, falling down, getting up, following the Master.

And so, the Apprentice said, "Yes, Master?"

And again, the Master bid him, "Come and die. Follow me."

And the Apprentice said, "Yes, Master."

The revolution was faithfulness. Faithfulness to the historic movement that brought together people of all ages and genders and colors and places, whether they were powerful or poor, academics or day laborers. Over and against those who distorted The Way, and in defiance of the flimsy faux spirituality of our own design.

Below were the digital pseudo-luminaries in their balsa wood cathedrals built like echo chambers to send their own voices back to them again and again, and the Apprentice would leave them to their threadbare patchwork spirituality, their hazy catchphrase theology of the god in the reflection. The wide road leads to death. Death to the wide road. Death to the gods made in our image, the golden calves of bailing out. Long is the way and hard, that out of hell leads up to light.

The way down was faster, the way up slower by a lifetime and more.

Death to deconstruction. To hell with the path of least resistance, the status quo. Death to the empty inherited religiousness of a plastic Christian culture, and death to the swinging pendulum that reacts against it with unthinking abandonment and pseudo-spirituality. Death to politicized faith and death to politicized deconversion. May God tear down the idols and infrastructures of the proud, be they televangelists or influencers, pulpits or podcasts.

Below was the deconstruction, but ahead was the movement—The Way. Against the storm, the Apprentice went with his blood thrumming in his heart and his mind. Below was the giving up. Ahead was the rebellion.

Faithfulness as an act of rebellion.

THANK YOU.

Thank you, Amanda Luedeke, my agent. It's been an emotional roller coaster. I was consistently grateful to have you as my copassenger.

Thank you, my very patient and encouraging editor, Kristin Fry.

Thank you, Katherine Chappell, Lindsay Danielson, Sarah De Mey, Joel Armstrong, Catherine DeVries, and everyone at Kregel.

Thank you, Patrick Porter, Michael Dumont, Gavin Bennett, and Matt Hughes; longtime first readers. D17.

Thank you, my generous friend and talented designer, Tyler Hanns.

Thank you, John Mark Comer, my mentor and my friend.

Thank you, Rick McKinley, Spiritual Director Supreme.

Thank you, Cameron Silsbee, Erik Peterson, Scott Bargaehr, Erik Tabinowski, Katie VanDomelen, Keana Zoradi, Levi Warren, Taylor Long, and Ariel Villaseñor, the staff, overseers, and deacons of Van City Church, for supporting me.

Thank you, my Van City community, including but not limited to Peter and Alla Nikiforov, Hannah Silsbee, Vanessa Porter, and Mike Jensen for your prayers, friendship, and support.

Thank you, Van City Church family, for having me.

Thank you, Beck, Isla, and Arlo. Smush and smash.

And thank you, Abigail. Forever.

Thank you, Reader. ourfathersweremodelsforgod.com password: notaband. Death to deconstruction.

NOTES

Foreword

1. Thomas Merton, *No Man Is an Island* (Boston: Shambhala, 2005), 35.
2. Singing—true story—songs that were intellectual rebuttals of both Nietzsche's nihilism and John Piper's Calvinism.

(Before We Begin)

1. Thomas Merton, *New Seeds of Contemplation* (Cambridge: New Directions, 1961), 180.

Chapter 1

1. "Showbread vs. Southern Baptists," Showbread, March 18, 2009, YouTube video, https://www.youtube.com/watch?v=H LQyuVoulaA.
2. Joshua Harris (@harrisjosh), Instagram, July 26, 2019, https://www.instagram.com/p/B0ZBrNLH2sl/?igshid=YmMyMTA2 M2y=/.
3. Stephen Eric Bronner, *Critical Theory: A Very Short Introduction* (New York: Oxford University Press, 2011), 1.
4. Gregory A. Boyd (@greg_boyd), Twitter, October 16, 2011, 5:59 p.m., https://twitter.com/greg_boyd?lang=en.

Chapter 3

1. David Sylvester, *The Brutality of Fact: Interviews with Francis Bacon* (New York: Thames & Hudson, 1980), 182.
2. I recommend *Unbreakable* by Andrew Wilson, *Shaped by the Word* by Robert Mulholland, *The Drama of Scripture* by Craig G. Bartholomew and Michael W. Goheen, *Why the Bible*

Matters by Mike Erre, *The Mission of God* by Christopher J. H. Wright, *A Walk Through the Bible* by Lesslie Newbigin, and everything created by The Bible Project (bibleproject.com).

3. The cartoon referenced is by Adam Zyglis, a Pulitzer Prize–winning American editorial cartoonist who works for *The Buffalo News* of Buffalo, New York.

4. "kataluō," in *Strong's Exhaustive Concordance of the Bible* (Peabody, MA: Hendrickson Publishers, 1988).

5. Andrew Wilson, *Unbreakable: What the Son of God Said About the Word of God* (La Grange, KY: 10Publishing, 2014), 12.

Chapter 4

1. "Official Video: Russell Brand Interviews Westboro Baptist Church," Russell Brand, November 27, 2012, YouTube video, 4:00, https://www.youtube.com/watch?v=OBA6qlHW8po.

2. Martin Luther King Jr., *Why Jesus Called a Man a Fool* (sermon, Mount Pisgah Missionary Baptist Church, Chicago, Illinois, August 27, 1967).

3. *Guinness World Records*, accessed January 27, 2021, https://www.guinnessworldrecords.com/world-records/best-selling-book-of-non-fiction.

4. James Packer, "Hermeneutics and Biblical Authority," *The Churchman* 81, no. 1 (Spring 1967): 20.

5. Tom Nichols, *The Death of Expertise: The Campaign Against Established Knowledge and Why it Matters* (New York: Oxford University Press, 2017), X.

6. This is not a metaphor. Jefferson used a razor blade and glue to mutilate a Bible into submission. You can see one of them on display at the Smithsonian National Museum of American History.

7. Brian Zahnd, "My Problem with the Bible," *Brian Zahnd* (blog), February 17, 2014, brianzahnd.com/2014/02/problem-bible/.

8. A. J. Swoboda, *After Doubt: How to Question Your Faith without Losing It* (Grand Rapids: Brazos Press, 2021), 53.

9. Swoboda, *After Doubt*, 55.

Chapter 5

1. Bret Easton Ellis, *Less Than Zero* (New York: Vintage Books, 2010), 127.

Chapter 6

1. Joanna Robinson, "What Would Actor Stephen Fry Say If He Met God? 'How Dare You'," *Vanity Fair*, February 3, 2015, https://www.vanityfair.com/hollywood/2015/02/stephen-fry-anti-god-rant.

2. Check out the Canons of the Second Council of Orange in AD 529, where the response to Augustine's idea of a God who ordains evil was, "We not only do not believe that any are fore-ordained to evil by the power of God, but even state with utter abhorrence that if there are those who want to believe so evil a thing, they are anathema." See *Canons of the Second Council of Orange* with an intr., tr. and notes by F.H. Woods (United Kingdom: n.p., 1882).

3. C. S. Lewis, *Mere Christianity* (San Francisco: HarperOne, 2009), 52–53.

4. Darwin Correspondence Project, "Letter no. 2814," accessed on September 7, 2021, https://www.darwinproject.ack.uk/letter/DCP-LETT-2814.xml.

5. Darwin Correspondence Project, "To J. D. Hooker on 13 July 1856," accessed on September 7, 2021, https://www.darwinproject.ack.uk/letter/DCP-LETT-1924.xml.

6. Gregory A. Boyd, *God at War: The Bible & Spiritual Conflict* (Downers Grove, IL: InterVarsity Press, 1997), 129.

7. Lewis, *Mere Christianity*, 52–53.

8. Gregory A. Boyd, "Why Is the World Still So Messed Up?" July 28, 2016, https://reknew.org/2016/07/world-still-messed/.

9. David Bentley Hart, *The Doors of the Sea: Where Was God in the Tsunami?* (Grand Rapids: Eerdmans, 2005), 91.

(Before We Continue)

1. Her name is Marsha M. Linehan.

Chapter 8

1. Karl P. Donfried, "The Imperial Cults of Thessalonica and Political Conflict in 1 Thessalonians," in *Paul and Empire: Religion and Power in Roman Imperial Society*, ed. Richard A. Horsley (Harrisburg: Trinity Press International, 1997), 216.

2. Accessed August 16, 2021, https://www.uscis.gov/citizenship /learn-about-citizenship/the-naturalization-interview-and-test /naturalization-oath-of-allegiance-to-the-united-states-of -america.

3. This was a lyric I'd borrowed from Georgia punk band Squad Five-0's song, "Our State Flag Sucks."

4. "CNN Late Edition with Wolf Blitzer," *CNN Late Edition with Wolf Blitzer*, CNN, October 24, 2004, http://transcripts .cnn.com/TRANSCRIPTS/0410/24/le.01.html.

5. "tassō," in *Strong's Exhaustive Concordance of the Bible* (Peabody, MA: Hendrickson Publishers, 1988).

6. Barna Group, "A New Generation Expresses Its Skepticism and Frustration with Christianity," September 21, 2007, https:// www.barna.com/research/a-new-generation-expresses-its -skepticism-and-frustration-with-christianity/.

Chapter 9

1. Agnieszka Tennant, "A 'Coward' Who Stayed to Help," *Christianity Today*, October 10, 2005, https://www.christianity today.com/ct/2005/octoberweb-only/42.0.html.

Chapter 10

1. Denny Burk, "Adultery or Rape? What Happened between David and Bathsheba?," *Denny Burk: A Commentary on Theology, Politics and Culture* (blog), October 9, 2019, https://www .dennyburk.com/adultery-or-rape-what-happened-between -david-and-bathsheba/.

2. Alexander Izuchukwu Abasili, "Was It Rape? The David and Bathsheba Pericope Re-Examined," *Vetus Testamentum* 61, no. 1 (2011): 1–15, http://www.jstor.org/stable/41308981.

3. *The Age of Spin: Dave Chappelle Live at the Hollywood Palladium*, directed by Stan Lathan (Pilot Boy Productions, 2017).

4. *Se7en*, directed by David Fincher (New Line Cinema, 1995).

5. Agnieszka Tennant, "A 'Coward' Who Stayed to Help," *Christianity Today*, October 10, 2005, https://www.christianity today.com/ct/2005/octoberweb-only/42.0.html.

6. Brennan Manning, *The Ragamuffin Gospel: Embracing the Unconditional Love of God* (Sisters, OR: Multnomah Books, 1990), 16–17.

7. Mother Teresa, *Mother Teresa: Come Be My Light: The Private Writings of the Saint of Calcutta*, ed. Brian Kolodiejchuk, (New York: Doubleday, 2007), 169–70.

8. Lizzy Goodman, "Trent Reznor," in *Difficult Artist with Lizzy Goodman*, podcast audio, May 12, 2021, https://podcasts.apple.com/us/podcast/trent-reznor/id1565264041?i=1000 521436310.

9. Jerome, *On Illustrious Men*, trans. Ernest Cushing Richardson (Philadelphia: Dalcassian Publishing Company, 2019), 6.

10. Joseph H. Hellerman, *When the Church Was a Family: Recapturing Jesus' Vision for Authentic Christian Community* (Nashville: B&H Academic, 2009), 1.

Chapter 11

1. Dorothy Day, *The Reckless Way of Love: Notes on Following Jesus*, ed. Carolyn Kurtz (Walden, NY: Plough Publishing House, 2017), 36.

Chapter 12

1. Katherine Dunn, *One Ring Circus: Dispatches from the World of Boxing* (Tuscon, AZ: Schaffner Press, Inc., 2009), 228–29.

2. "Tearful Weepy-Voiced Killer's 911 Calls," True Crime Magazine, May 20, 2015, YouTube video, https://www.youtube.com/watch?v=ItQpWcoJza0.

3. Aleister Crowley, *The Book of the Law* (Boston: Weiser Books, 2004), 13.

4. Eric Snider, "Jam Interviews Marilyn Manson," *Jam Magazine*, February 17, 1995, https://www.mansonwiki.com/wiki/Interview:Jam_Interviews_Marilyn_Manson.

5. *MTV Diary*, season 1, episode 6, "Jennifer Lopez," aired March 22, 2000, ViacomCBS Domestic Media Networks.

6. Albert Schweitzer, as quoted in Frederick Dale Bruner, *Matthew: A Commentary* (Grand Rapids: Eerdmans, 2004), 810.

7. Bruner, *Matthew*, 810.

8. Bruner, *Matthew*, 8.

9. Mark Sayers, *Reappearing Church: The Hope for Renewal in the Rise of Our Post-Christian Culture* (Chicago: Moody Publishers, 2019), 12.

10. Elizabeth Bird, "Top 100 Picture Books #85: The Giving Tree by Shel Silverstein." *A Fuse #8 Production*, May 18, 2012, blogs.slj.com/afuse8production/2012/05/18/top-100-picture-books-85-the-giving-tree-by-shel-silverstein/.

11. Meister Eckhart, as quoted in Thomas R. Kelly, *A Testament of Devotion* (San Francisco: HarperSanFrancisco, 1996), 8.

12. As quoted in Colleen M. Conway, *Behold the Man: Jesus and Greco-Roman Masculinity* (Oxford: Oxford University Press, 2008), 67.

13. Thomas Merton, *New Seeds of Contemplation* (New York: New Directions, 1972), 34.

14. Dietrich Bonhoeffer, *The Cost of Discipleship* (New York: Touchstone, 1995), 15.

15. Dallas Willard, *Renovation of the Heart: Putting on the Character of Christ* (Colorado Springs: NavPress, 2002), 64.

16. Ignatius of Loyola, as quoted in David G. Benner, *Surrender to Love: Discovering the Heart of Christian Spirituality* (Downers Grove, IL: InterVarsity Press, 2015), 66.

Chapter 13

1. Joan Didion, *The White Album* (New York: Farrar, Straus & Giroux, 2009), 11.

(Before We End)

1. Ronald Rolheiser, *Sacred Fire: A Vision for a Deeper Human and Christian Maturity* (New York: Image, 2014), 205–6.

2. Thomas Merton, *New Seeds of Contemplation* (Cambridge: New Directions, 1961), 180.